MW00789723

# THE ULTIMATE
# SPORTS TRIVIA BOOK

A COLLECTION OF FASCINATING STORIES,
AMAZING TRIVIA QUIZZES AND FUN FACTS
FOR SPORTS LOVERS!

## BILL O'NEILL

**ISBN: 978-1-64845-130-0**

Copyright © 2024 by LAK Publishing

ALL RIGHTS RESERVED

No part of this book may be reproduced, stored in a retrieval system, or transmitted in any form or by any means, electronic, mechanical, photocopying, recording, scanning, or otherwise, without the prior written permission of the publisher.

# DON'T FORGET YOUR FREE BOOK

GET THEM AT WWW.TRIVIABILL.COM

## GET THEM FOR FREE ON
## WWW.TRIVIABILL.COM

# CONTENTS

INTRODUCTION ................................................................1

CHAPTER 1: WORLD CHAMPIONSHIPS .....................................4

A Brief History of World Championships....................................5

Fun World Championships Facts...............................................7

Great World Championships Stories...........................................9

*Usain Bolt's Double* .............................................................9

*The 1969 IIHF World Ice Hockey Championships* ........................11

*Brazil's Beautiful Goal* ......................................................13

*Greece Topples the Americans* .............................................15

*Ohtani v. Trout* ................................................................17

*Armand Duplantis Dominates the Pole Vault* ............................19

A World Championships Quiz.................................................21

CHAPTER 2: TENNIS...........................................................24

A Brief History of Tennis.....................................................25

Fun Tennis Facts................................................................27

Great Tennis Stories...........................................................29

*Monica Seles Returns* ........................................................29

*Djokovic's Uneasy Rise*......................................................31

*Andre Agassi's Rise, Fall, and Rise*........................................33

*Serena Williams Breaks Through* ..........................................35

*Arthur Ashe Paves the Path in the USA* ........................................37

*Esther Vergeer's Wheelchair Tennis Dominance* ........................39

A Tennis Quiz........................................................................................41

**CHAPTER 3: BOXING AND MIXED MARTIAL ARTS..........44**

A Brief History of Combat Sports....................................................45

Fun Combat Sports Facts....................................................................47

Great Combat Sports Stories..............................................................48

*Rumble in the Jungle* ....................................................................48

*Mayweather vs. Pacquiao*..............................................................50

*Tyson Captivates and Crashes* ....................................................52

*Jon Jones' Troubled Reign* ..........................................................54

*Anderson Silva*................................................................................57

*The Thrilla in Manila* ....................................................................59

A Boxing and MMA Quiz ..................................................................61

**CHAPTER 4: ICE HOCKEY .............................................64**

A Brief History of Ice Hockey..........................................................65

Fun Ice Hockey Facts ........................................................................67

Great Ice Hockey Stories ..................................................................68

*Lemieux's Return* ..........................................................................68

*Paul Kariya Gets Up* ....................................................................70

*Gordie Howe's Long Career* ........................................................72

*The Miracle on Ice* ........................................................................74

*The Red Wings Repeat* ..................................................................77

*Bobby Baun Plays Injured*............................................................79

An Ice Hockey Quiz.............................................................81

**CHAPTER 5: BASKETBALL**.......................................**83**

A Brief History of Basketball........................................84

Fun Basketball Facts .....................................................86

Great Basketball Stories ...............................................87

*Magic Johnson Takes Over* ........................................87

*The Flu Game* ............................................................89

*Dirk Beats the Big 3* ..................................................91

*Kobe and Shaq Break Up*...........................................93

*Larry's Incredible Putback* ........................................95

*The Dream Team* .......................................................97

A Basketball Quiz..........................................................99

**CHAPTER 6: EUROPEAN FOOTBALL** ..................... **102**

A Brief History of European Football......................... 103

Fun European Football Facts....................................... 105

Great European Football Stories................................. 106

*Zidane Volleys a Championship* ............................... 106

*The 2005 Champions League Final* .......................... 108

*Watford's Final Chance* ........................................... 110

*The 1994 World Cup Final* ....................................... 112

*Aguero's Last-Minute Goal* ..................................... 114

*The 1988 FA Cup Final* ............................................ 116

A European Football Quiz........................................... 118

**CHAPTER 7: AMERICAN FOOTBALL**...................... **121**

A Short History of American Football ........................................122

Fun American Football Facts .....................................................124

Great American Football Stories ...............................................125

    *Boise State's Tricky Win* ........................................................125

    *The Helmet Catch* .................................................................127

    *The Perfect Season* ...............................................................129

    *The 2013 Iron Bowl* ..............................................................131

    *The Immaculate Reception* ...................................................133

    *One Yard Short* .....................................................................135

An American Football Quiz ........................................................137

**CHAPTER 8: BASEBALL** .............................................................**140**

A Short History of Baseball .......................................................141

Fun Baseball Facts .....................................................................143

Great Baseball Stories ...............................................................144

    *The Miracle Mets* ..................................................................144

    *Jackie Robinson* .....................................................................146

    *The Cubs' Curse* .....................................................................148

    *The Shot Heard 'Round the World* .........................................150

    *Red Sox Down 3-0* .................................................................152

    *The 1998 Home Run Race* .....................................................154

A Baseball Quiz .........................................................................156

**CONCLUSION** ..............................................................................**159**

**SOLUTIONS** .................................................................................**161**

# INTRODUCTION

Sports around the world have greatly benefited from the boom of technology over the past 80 years, creating superstars known in almost every corner of the planet.

Fans of every kind of sport have consumed knowledge about their favorite games and favorite athletes, helping sports grow and spread.

Of course, sports as a form of entertainment is not a new concept. There is some historical debate about the first evidence of friendly competition in physical events, with several examples of pre-historic cave paintings depicting sports like wrestling, running, and archery.

Over the centuries of human history, sports have evolved into a pure form of entertainment, moving away from the war training it often mimicked and into games of athleticism and skill.

Along the way, sports of all kinds have grown and developed, giving fans of the competition plenty of variety to experience and enjoy.

With all that variety comes a potential wealth of knowledge. Many individuals pick a favorite sport and learn as much as they can, but few are able to master trivia about multiple sports.

This book seeks to both deliver information and test your recall on a wide range of sports. Each chapter will provide a short history of the sport or competition, along with some fun facts about the game. Then, your knowledge of the sport will be tested with ten questions, to see if your 'fandom' of the game is true.

The challenge in this book is that each chapter will focus on a different sport, and a wide variety will be covered. Boxing and other combat sports will be included, along with European football, American football, and more of the most popular games on Earth.

For example, do you know which footballer has scored more goals for his country than any other player in the history of the sport?

Now, European football is arguably the most popular sport in the world, so that may have been an easy answer for you. Don't worry, more challenging questions are coming!

This book will also cover Olympic events, golf, cricket, and baseball, sports that are very popular in large pockets of the world but are not exactly worldwide games yet, so the trivia is a little more niche.

These sports may not be as popular as others where you live, which means there is more for you to learn about these great sports that have earned so much attention from other fans.

The athletes who have played these sports accomplished great things during their time in competition. Those accomplishments are worth celebrating and remembering, as many of the milestones are unlikely to be matched for many years to come.

Their achievements should be immortalized in human history, even if sports are not as consequential as worldwide politics or scientific breakthroughs.

These great players have entertained the world for millennia, and sportspeople will continue to entertain with their skill and dedication to their sport.

So, without further ado, let's jump into the trivia and learn something new about these amazing sports!

# CHAPTER 1
# WORLD CHAMPIONSHIPS

# A Brief History of World Championships

While many people would think of the Olympic Games as the first world championship contests in human history, the origins of world championships are actually much more recent.

After all, most historians do not consider the first Olympic games to be world championships, as they did not feature enough athletes from around the world. To gather a truly worldwide field of competitors, there needed to be enough developed countries with skilled individuals, not to mention the communication and logistics required to organize an event of such a scale.

As such, the first well-documented world championships took place in the 1700s. According to most historians, real tennis (the racquet game from which modern tennis originates) holds the distinction as having the oldest documented men's world championship.

As the world advanced into the 1800s, several more world championships were organized and held, though entirely in competitions that only invited men to compete. Sports such as billiards, speed skating, weightlifting, cycling, and figure skating all held men's world championships before the beginning of the 20th century.

Major sports such as ice hockey and European football began world championship contests in 1920 and 1930, respectively, while the first world championship open to any gender actually occurred in auto racing. The World Manufacturer's Championship began in 1925, though it only lasted for a couple of years. Motorcycling and gliding were the next two sports to have an open world championship, beginning in 1936 and 1937. Both of those events still take place to the present day.

In terms of popularity, the FIFA World Cup is by far the most watched world championship competition, followed by the Cricket World Cup, both open and women's competitions.

The popularity of world championship sports only continues to grow as technology allows more athletes to compete and more fans to tune in and follow the action.

# Fun World Championships Facts

1. Brazil is the only country to have competed in every single iteration of the FIFA World Cup. The next closest team is Germany, which missed two competitions.

2. The 2019 Cricket World Cup marks the only tournament final that ended tied after both the regular play and super over. England won that championship based on boundary count.

3. The Women's Cricket World Cup holds the distinction of being the sport's longest-running world championship, as it held its first contest in 1973, two years before the first men's iteration.

4. Usain Bolt of Jamaica holds more World Athletics Championships gold medals than any other man, with 11 and 8 Olympic Gold Medals (he had to hand back the 9th). Allyson Felix of the United States leads all women in the same category, with 14 and 7 Olympic Gold Medals

5. Sweden has competed in the top division of the Ice Hockey World Championships more often than any other country, with 82 appearances. Canada leads all countries with 28 gold medals in those competitions.

6. Simone Biles of the United States has won 23 gold medals in the World Artistic Gymnastics Championships, 14 more than the next closest athlete on the all-time list.

7. When it comes to the World Table Tennis Championships, which has been held regularly since 1926, China has won more than double the medals of the next closest country. Their 433.5 medals are 233 more than Hungary, which is in second place on the all-time list. Since 1975, the Chinese women's team has only lost twice.

8. Italy is the most successful country in the World Fencing Championships, with its participants having captured 122 gold medals since 1921. No other country has more than 100 golds, and only three other countries have more than 60.

9. While the United States has earned more medals than any other country in the World Figure Skating Championships, Norway's Sonja Henie holds the record for most women's singles titles, with ten, and Ulrich Salchow of Sweden has ten men's titles, also a record.

10. The World All-round Speed Skating Championships have been held since 1893, with the Netherlands leading all countries with 57 golds.

# Great World Championships Stories

## Usain Bolt's Double

Capturing a world record on one of the biggest stages of international competition is a rare feat, but it is even rarer to achieve such a feat twice in one competition. When Usain Bolt accomplished this in 2009, he captured the attention of much of the world in the process.

Let's set the scene in Berlin for the 2009 World Championships in Athletics. Usain Bolt was entering the competition as the world record holder in both the 100-metres (meters) and 200-metre races, both set during his performance at the 2008 Olympic Games. His 100-metre time at the Olympics had broken his previous record from two months earlier, and the world wondered just how many times he could shock the competition. Bolt was a loud personality, playing into his newfound fame and entertaining audiences with his confidence, drawing even more attention to his exploits.

Exactly one year after his incredible Olympic performance, Bolt was on the track once again. Though he had been in a car accident a few months before the world championships, he had recovered from minor surgery and was looking to keep his crown as the "fastest man on Earth."

First came the 100-metre competition. Bolt eased through the qualifying heats and prepared for the final. Waiting for him was American Tyson Gay, who was also running well heading into the competition. Usain Bolt was not intimidated, and his performance showed that he was still hungry to improve. Bolt won the race, crossing the line with a time of 9.58 seconds. It was a new world record for Bolt, taking 0.11 seconds off his previous time. It was the largest amount of time taken from a world record since the introduction of electronic timing. As of 2023, this record still stands.

Then, in the 200-metre race, Bolt sought to continue his winning ways. However, there were three other competitors capable of running the race in less than 19.90 seconds. There have never been that many competitors capable of that feat all facing off in a world championship race. Bolt had his work cut out for him.

Still, he had been training, working particularly on his starting reaction times, and he wanted to win. Bolt went to work and dominated the field in the 200-metre final, finishing with a time of 19.19 seconds, another world record shattered. He won by the largest margin in the history of the world championships, beating Alonso Edward of Panama by 0.62 seconds.

Usain Bolt had beaten his previous record by the same margin as his record-shattering performance earlier in the competition: 0.11 seconds!

Usain Bolt had set the world on fire with his performances. As of 2023, both of his records from the 2009 World Championships remain unbeaten. In a time when world records fall every few years as athletes continue to improve, Usain Bolt's records remain seemingly untouchable.

One of his competitors in the 200-metre race, American Shawn Crawford, told interviewers that he was amazed by Bolt's performance, saying, "I felt like I was in a video game. That guy was moving - fast."

It may be quite a long time before anyone can top what Usain Bolt accomplished in 2009. Even if those records fall, Bolt's performance at that world championship in Berlin will remain a story worth telling.

# The 1969 IIHF World Ice Hockey Championships

When athletes are tasked with representing their home country in an international competition, it can lead to emotionally and politically charged moments, depending on the issues dominating at home and abroad. This was the case during the 1969 World Ice Hockey Championships for one team in particular: Czechoslovakia.

In August 1968, the Soviet Union invaded and quickly occupied Czechoslovakia, seeking to quash movements in the country that sought to create distance between their country and the Soviet regime. While many citizens did their best to peacefully protest the occupation by doing things such as giving incorrect directions to Soviet soldiers, it seemed as though the country could do little to fight back against such a powerful foe.

The World Ice Hockey Championships were scheduled to take place in Spring 1969. Normally, this would be another opportunity for the Soviet Union to demonstrate their power. At that stage, the Soviet Union had won every iteration of the event dating back to 1963. They were looking to win their seventh tournament in a row. To do so, they would need to defeat Czechoslovakia, a squad that had won two bronze medals and three silver medals during the Soviets' string of six straight golds.

Victories against the Soviets were hard to come by during this streak. Sweden beat them once in 1963, and Czechoslovakia defeated them once in 1968, but those two losses were the only ones during the Soviets' gold medal streak.

Then, amazingly, on March 21, 1969, the Czechoslovakia national team defeated the Soviet team by a score of 2-0. It was a monumental victory that gave the Czechoslovakia team a small outside chance to win the tournament. They would need help, though.

After all, each team was playing each other twice, and no team had beaten the Soviets twice in one tournament before. Still, the Czechoslovakia national team was determined, likely inspired by what was happening back at home, to get the job done. One week later, the unthinkable happened. On March 28, 1969, Czechoslovakia defeated the Soviet Union again, 4-3!

It was a massive moment in international ice hockey, and it inspired the citizens of the winning country to celebrate the team's victory. It also inspired many of the citizens to turn their celebration into a protest.

It is estimated that 500,000 citizens took to the streets around the country, particularly in the city of Prague, to celebrate the team's victories. In a moment that is now known as the Czechoslovak Hockey Riots, fans cheered with such phrases as, "No tanks were there so they lost!" They also made signs that had messages like "Czechoslovakia 4 – Occupation forces 3!".

Most of the protests were peaceful, but there was still a lasting effect. The Soviet Union took the protests as a sign that leadership in Czechoslovakia needed to change, moving away from liberalization and back toward the communist practices of the Soviet Union.

The Czechoslovakia national team's performance in that tournament was viewed as a silent form of protest against the Soviets, and while the Soviet Union still prevailed in that tournament thanks to a stronger goals-for/goals-against record, the Czechoslovak squad showed that they could fight back.

# Brazil's Beautiful Goal

The world championship known as the FIFA World Cup is the most popular competition on the planet. While football is the most popular sport in the world thanks to its accessibility, the World Cup gets its popularity from the extremely high level of play the top teams demonstrate on the pitch.

In all the years the tournament has been held, few moments have showcased the quality of play and individual skill like the 1970 Brazil national team. Led by Pele, Jairzinho, Rivellino, Tostao, and Carlos Alberto, many considered Brazil to be the favorites heading into the tournament.

Though they were favored to win, the second match of their tournament was against the defending champions, England. It was a tightly contested first half, but the second half was a much more open contest. Jairzinho scored in the 59th minute to give Brazil the lead, and though England had several opportunities to equalize, they could not find a goal.

Both teams would advance to the knockout stage of the tournament after defeating Czechoslovakia and Romania in Group 3. With only three matches between Brazil and the championship, fans waited expectantly to see if any of their opponents could make the matches interesting.

In the quarterfinals, the Brazilian side jumped out to a quick lead over Peru thanks to a Rivellino goal in the 11th minute. Their lead was doubled just four minutes later when Tostao added a goal. Gallardo responded for Peru in the 28th minute, but Brazil would continue to pour it on in the second half. They scored in the 52nd minute, conceded a goal in the 70th minute, but increased their lead to two goals once more in the 75th minute to win the match and advance.

In the semifinals, they dispatched Uruguay after falling behind in the first half, thanks to an equalizer just before halftime, then two more goals in the second half.

Throughout the tournament, Brazil won every single match they played, often winning by more than one goal, as they cruised to the Final, where they faced Italy for a chance to win their country's third World Cup title.

One goal in particular demonstrated just how beautiful the game can be. Forward player Tostao won possession of the ball in his own half, about 100 yards away from Italy's goal. Passes between him, Brito, Pele, Clodoaldo, and Gerson started the buildup of the play, before Clodoaldo took it upon himself to dribble between four Italian defenders. Clodoaldo then passed to Rivellino, who sent the ball up the sideline to Jairzinho. Another pass to the middle once more found Pele, who knew where his teammate would be along the right side.

Without looking, Pele put the ball into that space, where Carlos Alberto was able to run onto the pass and fire a one-touch shot, low and too hard for the Italian keeper to get a hand on it.

Nine players on the Brazilian squad touched that ball before it was in the back of the net. There was nothing the Italians could do, and the goal gave Brazil a three-goal lead late in the contest, sealing the World Cup victory for one of the most talented teams in World Cup history.

It was a strong team at a time when scoring and attacking were encouraged. Jairzinho remains the only player to score in every match of a World Cup tournament.

To this day, many consider that Brazilian side to be one of the best of all time.

# Greece Topples the Americans

Many stories have been told about National Basketball Association players and their successes in international competition, beginning with the Dream Team of 1992. Ever since NBA players joined international play on a large scale, the Americans have always been favored to win. Imagine the shock, then, when they faced stiff competition during the 2006 FIBA World Championships.

Few believed that many teams had a chance against the American roster in 2006. The team included names like LeBron James, Chris Bosh, Carmelo Anthony, Dwyane Wade, and Chris Paul. It may not have been as packed with superstars as the famous squad from the early 90s, but it was still quite formidable.

They proved their strength in the group stage, winning their five games by a total of 115 points. For comparison, Spain exited the group stage with five wins and a +140-point differential, while Greece won their five games with a +46.

Australia was the Americans' first opponent in the knockout stage, and the United States did not let up. They defeated the Australian team by 40 points, easily advancing to face Germany. Greece won their game against China, then defeated France to advance to the semifinals. The Americans beat the Germans by 20, setting up a match against the strong Greece team.

Though the Americans jumped out to a 20-14 lead in the first quarter, the veteran Greek team stormed back in the second quarter, scoring 31 points and holding a four-point lead at halftime.

The Greece team, led by Vassilis Spanoulis with 22 points and Theodoros Papaloukas with 12 assists, kept finding ways to get to the basket. The Americans could not keep up with the speed and technique of Greece's big men, who were able to utilize pick-and-roll plays for much of the second half to great effect.

By the final minute of the game, Greece was up by seven points and did not relinquish their lead. The final score was 101-95, and the Americans had fallen to a strong team of veteran players.

It was a groundbreaking moment in international basketball, putting the world on notice that not all of the best players are from the United States. It also showed that a team of veteran players could overcome more talented individuals, as long as they played as a team.

At the end of the tournament, though, Greece came down from their emotional victory with a loss to Spain in the final. The United States won their consolation game, giving them the bronze medal.

For the American team, it was a wake-up call. After their disappointing showings in 2004 and 2006, they were determined to recapture the magic of the Dream Team. Thanks in part to Greece's fantastic victory in the FIBA World Cup of 2006, the American Redeem Team of 2008 was born, another famous moment on the international stage.

Still, Greece's victory was a great one, and although they couldn't win the tournament, they defeated the favorites.

# Ohtani v. Trout

The World Baseball Classic is not one of the oldest world championship tournaments, but it has quickly become one of the most celebrated, as teams from around the world compete for their countries, often against some of their own teammates from the professional leagues.

In the 2023 edition of the tournament, the big news from the American team was a wave of big-name players announcing their intent to represent their country. Mike Trout was the biggest name on that list, considering he was one of the most decorated players in Major League Baseball at the time.

There was another squad that had assembled an all-star level roster for the tournament, and that was Japan. The most decorated player on that team was Shohei Ohtani, the 2021 AL MVP. And get this: Trout and Ohtani were teammates in Major League Baseball, as they both played for the Los Angeles Angels!

And in the final game of the tournament, this ended up mattering a whole lot. The 2023 World Baseball Classic Final was a matchup between the American and Japanese teams that had been so highly regarded before the tournament began. Though few could imagine a scenario where the game would be decided in a showdown between Ohtani and Trout, that is exactly what happened.

It was the top of the ninth inning. Two outs. The United States was trailing 3–2, and Mike Trout was the team's last hope. He had hit a double in the first inning of the contest, but he had not registered a hit in his other three at-bats. Shohei Ohtani was on the mound in relief, though he was usually a starting pitcher.

It was an epic moment no one had expected.

Ohtani opened the at-bat with a breaking ball that went low for ball 1. The crowd in the stadium buzzed in anticipation as the showdown continued.

Then, a 100-mph fastball right down the middle. Trout took a swing at it, but he missed. The count was back to even. The commentators mused that, "Baseball has already won" because of the dream scenario in front of their eyes.

A second 100-mph fastball missed the outside edge of the plate, putting Trout ahead in the count. Ohtani was not flustered. A third-straight 100-mph fastball blown by Trout once again evened the count and put the Americans one strike from defeat, the Japanese one strike from a championship.

Then, a 102-mph fastball outside and into the dirt resulted in a full count. Both players were at their limit, unable to make any more mistakes. The crowd swelled in anticipation once again, knowing they were about to witness baseball history one way or another.

Then, Ohtani moved away from the fastball, and the breaking ball at 87 mph fooled Trout into a reaching swing. He was unable to get any contact on the ball, and the game was over. Japan had clinched the championship!

Both players were all-stars in the biggest baseball league in the world, and they were teammates in that league. But only one, Shohei Ohtani, would be returning to Los Angeles with a trophy in hand.

# Armand Duplantis Dominates the Pole Vault

In February 2020, a young Swedish American athlete named Armand "Mondo" Duplantis made pole vaulting history by breaking the world record held by Renaud Lavillenie. It was a record that had lasted almost six years, and Lavillenie had replaced a ten-year-old record himself, so such record-breaking vaults were a rare occurrence indeed.

Anyone who knew Duplantis as a younger athlete was likely not surprised. Both of his parents were athletes, and they were his primary trainers as he grew up. He was provided the tools to succeed, and he took the opportunity.

Though Duplantis was young, just 20 years old when he set the world record of 6.17 meters, few expected him to continue breaking the record with regularity - but he did.

One of his biggest record-breaking moments came during the 2022 World Athletics Championships in Oregon, USA. Armando had a slight scare early in the competition when he missed his first attempt at 5.87 meters, but he recovered and successfully made his second attempt.

With his nearest opponent only jumping a 5.94-meter height, Duplantis was essentially competing against himself for his final few jumps. The crowd watched in anticipation, everyone wondering just how high he would go. At this point in his career, he had already set the world record four times. The question was whether he had reached his limit or if he had more to give.

The crowd was electric as the sun began to set, casting long shadows across the field. Every other competitor in every other event was done for the day. It was the last attempt in the last event of the entire World Championship.

With successful vaults at 6.00 and 6.06, Duplantis decided to use his final height selection to attempt a vault of 6.21 meters. It would set the world record by 0.01 meters if he was successful. He had been jumping well, but the entire stadium was anxious to see if he could do it.

On his first attempt, he came up short. The crowd knew he had two more attempts, and they wanted to support him to victory. As Duplantis prepared to begin his second attempt, he led the crowd in a slow clap to set the stage.

As Duplantis began his runup, it was evident that he had the strength to reach the height, but would his execution match it?

Duplantis vaulted and easily cleared the bar, sending the crowd into cheers. It was a fitting end to the World Championships, setting a world record and sending the crowd home happy.

For Armand Duplantis, it was another notch in his world record belt, though he was eager to prove that he was not done. In February 2023, Duplantis added another hundredth of a meter to the record, then added another in September 2023, moving the record to 6.23 meters.

Most recently, in April 2024, Duplantis moved the record to 6.24 meters during a competition in Xiamen, China.

Duplantis' dominance has been steady and unquestionable. As of his most recent record, Duplantis is 24 years old, giving him plenty of opportunities to add to his incredible performances.

# A World Championships Quiz

Here are ten questions to further test your knowledge of world championships. The answer key for these questions can be found at the back of the book.

1. Jarmila Kratochvilova set two records at the inaugural World Athletics Championships in 1983, and those records still stand today. Which races were they?

   A. 100 meters and 200 meters
   B. 200 meters and 400 meters
   C. 400 meters and 800 meters
   D. 800 meters and 1,500 meters

2. In the FIBA Basketball World Cup tournaments, no player has averaged more points through a tournament than who?

   A. Oscar Schmidt
   B. Nikos Galis
   C. Shin Dong-pa
   D. Luis Scola

3. Which team has lost more games at FIFA World Cup competitions than any other team?

   A. Argentina
   B. Mexico
   C. Germany
   D. Serbia

4. As of 2023, which is the only team to lose four FIFA World Cup Finals?

   A. Argentina
   B. Netherlands

C. Brazil

D. Germany

5. **Which Soviet Union player is the only one to have collected 13 medals from IIHF Hockey World Championships?**

   A. Vladislav Tretiak

   B. Alexander Ragulin

   C. Alexander Maltsev

   D. Vladimir Petrov

6. **As of 2023, who is the only player to have multiple World Baseball Classic MVP awards?**

   A. Shohei Ohtani

   B. Daisuke Matsuzaka

   C. Fernando Rodney

   D. Carlos Beltran

7. **Which swimmer has collected 33 medals, more than any other athlete at the World Aquatics Championships?**

   A. Katie Ledecky

   B. Svetlana Romashina

   C. Natalia Ishchenko

   D. Michael Phelps

8. **Great Britain's Johnathan Edwards holds the world record in the triple jump, set during the World Athletics Championships in which year?**

   A. 1991

   B. 1995

   C. 2001

   D. 2007

9. **The Thomas Cup is an international world championship competition for which of these sports?**

A. Billiards

B. Cricket

C. Badminton

D. Cycling

**10.** **As of 2024, which team has the best all-time winning percentage during the ICC Men's Cricket World Cup?**

A. Australia

B. India

C. South Africa

D. New Zealand

# CHAPTER 2
# TENNIS

# A Brief History of Tennis

A direct descendant of real tennis, lawn tennis is the sport many think of when it comes to the word. While the origins of tennis are often traced to the 12th century, modern lawn tennis has a much more recent birthdate, as it split away from real tennis in the mid-1700s.

After about 100 years, the first tennis club was founded in 1872: The Leamington Tennis Club. This was only three years before the sport was introduced to Wimbledon, meaning that the game was soon to spread quickly.

Its spread was also said to have been assisted by Mary Ewing Outerbridge bringing the game back to the United States after having played it in Bermuda in 1874. Some argue that this account is inaccurate, however, and that Dr. James Dwight introduced the game to the United States in 1874 while playing in Massachusetts.

Regardless, once the game was established, championships were quickly organized, often to help clubs raise money. Wimbledon held their first championship in 1877, and the holding of these tournaments encouraged those organizers to quickly develop a standard set of rules for everyone to use. Four years later, the U.S. National Championship debuted in 1881, later becoming the U.S. Open in 1968.

The Championnat de France debuted in 1891, using clay and sand courts until switching to clay in 1909. The Davis Cup began in 1900, though it only featured the USA and Great Britain before quickly expanding. The Australasian Championships began in 1905, later becoming known as the Australian Open.

Continuing its quick expansion and growth, the game of tennis was strengthened even further in 1913 when 12 national tennis associations came to an agreement to form the International Lawn Tennis Federation. Eleven years later, in 1924, that federation introduced the ruleset that has largely gone unchanged since.

There were several attempts to create professional circuits, but due to the rules regarding the major tournaments, anyone who went pro and was paid for their play could not compete, as the major tournaments were considered amateur only.

Therefore, professional players would go on head-to-head tours, as these paid much better than pro tournaments did. There were professional championships established and held as early as the late 1920s, and some of those tournaments still exist today, though they have been downgraded in terms of their status as major events.

In 1968, the Grand Slam tournaments agreed to allow professional players to enter, thus beginning the Open Era of tennis. A few years later, in 1972, the Association of Tennis Professionals, or the ATP, was founded to help protect players from associations and promoters who sought to unfairly profit from them.

The ATP took over as the governing body of pro tennis in 1990, leading to the establishment of the ATP Tour. This tour is how many tennis fans now get to see tennis today.

# Fun Tennis Facts

1.  Jean Borotra, Henri Cochet, Rene Lacoste, and Jacques Brugnon were known as the Four Musketeers. They were four French players who dominated the tennis scene from 1924 to 1933, winning multiple championships between them.

2.  Don Budge became the first player in tennis history to win all four major titles in one year, a feat that he accomplished in 1938. Maureen Connolly was the next to achieve this feat in women's singles, in 1953.

3.  Australia won the Davis Cup 15 times in 18 years during the 1950s and 60s, a dominating run for one country, highlighted by Margaret Court winning the Grand Slam in 1970.

4.  Bjorn Borg won the French Open six times between 1974 and 1981. He also won Wimbledon five times in a row from 1976 to 1980.

5.  American woman Chris Evert won at least one Grand Slam title per year for 13 years in a row from 1974 to 1986, a record unmatched to this day. Her run ended thanks to the emergence of Steffi Graf, who would go on to dominate the game for a decade.

6.  The shortest Grand Slam final match was only 32 minutes of playing time, as Steffi Graf defeated Natasha Zvereva in straight sets to capture the 1988 French Open title. The shortest men's Grand Slam final was 36 minutes at Wimbledon in 1881.

7.  Novak Djokovic holds the record for most Grand Slam titles with 24. Rafael Nadal holds 22 titles and Roger Federer has 20.

8.  Monica Seles is the only tennis player to win eight Grand Slam titles before turning 20 years old. Steffi Graf is second

on that list with six. Rafael Nadal is the only male competitor with more than one Grand Slam before age 20.

9. The longest tennis match ever played lasted 11 hours and 5 minutes. It took place in 2010 during the first round of Wimbledon between John Isner and Nicolas Mahut.

10. Martina Navratilova collected an astonishing 354 tournament titles during her career, which lasted more than 30 years. Chris Evert is second on that list, and she only has 189 titles.

# Great Tennis Stories

## Monica Seles Returns

The early 1990s were some of the most entertaining years in women's tennis. Steffi Graf had cemented herself as the best player in the world during the late 80s, and her reign was being challenged by a young Monica Seles.

Seles won her first Grand Slam title in 1990 at only 16 years old and was the youngest to ever win the French Open. By the time she turned 20 years old, she had won eight major singles titles, earning herself the year-end number one ranking two years in a row.

It was a jarring challenge to Graf, who had enjoyed overwhelming success before Seles' arrival. However, this exciting rivalry was overshadowed when an April 1993 match between the pair took an ugly turn. While Seles was sitting on her bench for a short rest between games, a mentally unstable fan jumped onto the court and stabbed Seles in the back, between her shoulder blades, with a nine-inch knife.

It was a severe injury. Seles needed months to physically recover from what happened, but she needed even longer to overcome the mental strain. Fear and anxiety kept her from the game she loved for two years.

During that time, Graf continued to win Grand Slams and remained the top player in women's tennis. Many in the tennis world wondered if Seles would ever return, and others questioned whether Graf would have been so successful if her top rival had been healthy.

Regardless, much of that talk ended when Monica Seles returned to competitive tennis in 1995. Though she never recaptured the momentum and near-dominance she had enjoyed before her injury, she did find some limited success on the court. She even won one more major title, the 1996 Australian Open, defeating Anke Huber in straight sets.

Looking back, it seems unfair to both Steffi Graf and Monica Seles that events played out as they did. Seles lost prime years and also her confidence on the court, things that could never be recovered. Graf had to deal with the tennis world turning against her for something out of her control. After all, she had not committed the act against Seles.

It did not help, though, that the man who stabbed Seles proclaimed himself to be a fan of Graf's, as if he had done it to help her cause.

Still, both women enjoyed success at tennis' highest levels, even if Seles' time at the top was short-lived. Graf was going to be a great player regardless of what happened, so it is only appropriate to celebrate both players for their accomplishments, and not focus on what could have, or should have, been.

# Djokovic's Uneasy Rise

When the average person thinks of tennis players, they might picture a young individual in a wealthy family who is given plenty of opportunities to find success. After all, tennis is often played in country clubs, where wealthy individuals congregate.

This background, though, does not belong to the man considered by many to be the best tennis player of all time, Novak Djokovic.

Novak Djokovic needed to train as a young player to develop his skills, just as any professional player would need to do. However, when Novak was a teen, his homeland of Serbia was involved in a war. Serbia was part of Yugoslavia at the time, and the Yugoslav wars made it difficult for Novak, his trainers, and his friends to find places that were safe enough to train without worrying about the bombs dropping overhead.

That is not even mentioning the amount of mental stress one has to endure when living near a war zone. It cannot be good for the brain to live so close to death and destruction at all times, always wondering if the next bomb is coming your way.

Yet, Novak found a way to endure. He used the fear and mental stress as motivation. He knew he could use tennis as his ticket to escape all of the suffering and fear. With that motivation, he continued to work.

For training, Novak and his friends often practiced in an abandoned swimming pool. As it turns out, practicing in a swimming pool can have a noticeable effect on your game. One of the ways that Novak was limited by practicing in a pool is that his coaches did not allow cross-court shots. The coaches wanted to prevent players from sprinting head-first into a concrete wall while trying to chase down a shot across the court.

Instead, Novak got plenty of practice hitting shots down the line, something he has often utilized in his professional tennis matches.

Soon enough, Novak proved to his coaches that he was good enough to continue moving forward with a career in tennis, so he was sent to Germany to continue his training. There, Novak played on real tennis courts without living in fear of war at his doorstep.

Of course, Novak overcame everything from his youth to become the top tennis player in the world. He used his life experiences to strengthen his tennis game. Not many players can say that they learned how to play while under threat of a bomb dropping on them, and Novak reasons that this is why he can keep himself calm during the biggest moments in a match. After all, a tennis match is nothing compared to war.

As of 2024, Novak Djokovic has collected 24 Grand Slam titles, the most among all men's tennis players all-time. He has won ten Australian Open titles, seven Wimbledon titles, four U.S. Open titles, and three French Open titles. He also leads all players in money earned on tour, with over $180 million.

He found success through hard work and determination, even in the face of death.

# Andre Agassi's Rise, Fall, and Rise

The odds of becoming the best tennis player in the world are not great. The odds are even greater, then, to become the greatest player, then lose it all, only to gain it all back. This is what happened to Andre Agassi, one of the biggest tennis stars of the 1990s.

As a young player, many people around Andre Agassi knew that he had the chance to be something special in the tennis world. He was winning youth championships by age 12. He spent many of his teenage years training under Nick Bollettieri in Florida, USA, as the coach had offered Agassi a free ride at his training camp after seeing Agassi's potential.

Professionally, Agassi won his first match at age 16, and one year later, at the age of 17, he was ranked 25th in the world. From there, he skyrocketed up the rankings. His first major championship came at Wimbledon in 1992, and he became the top-ranked player in the world in April 1995. Although he did not keep that placement for very long, as he and Pete Sampras battled for supremacy in men's tennis, no one questioned the skill and athleticism of Andre Agassi during the early and mid-1990s.

Two years later, though, Agassi failed a drug test. He told the tennis association that it was an error, that there must have been some sort of confusion with his assistant, who had given him a drink with unknown contents. The truth, though, was that Agassi was struggling.

Players around him whispered and gossiped about his drug issue, and Andre's game suffered as he tried to quit the drug in secret. By the end of the 1997 season, Andre had fallen to 141st in the world rankings. The world of tennis saw his decline and believed his career was pretty much finished. After all, he had been in the game for a decade, and it would be difficult to overcome whatever was hurting his game.

Agassi could have walked away with his winnings and called it a career, but he decided he had more to give. In 1998, he worked on a new training and conditioning program, getting him back into shape and focused on tennis. He entered tournaments for players ranked outside the top 50, called the Challenger Series.

By the end of the 1998 season, with five tournament victories throughout the season, Agassi was ranked sixth in the world. His move from 110th to sixth made it the biggest jump into the top ten in a single season.

One year later, Agassi completed his career Grand Slam with a two-set-down comeback against Andrei Medvedev to win the French Open. This also completed what is known as the Super Slam: all four majors, an Olympic gold, and a year-end championship. He is the only male player to complete this feat.

At the end of the 1999 season, Agassi was the top player in the world once again. His great play continued for a few more years, cementing him as one of the best to ever play the sport. Few could have come back as strong as he did.

# Serena Williams Breaks Through

When a young player begins their march up the tennis rankings, it can be difficult to guess where their ascent will come to a stop. Will they run out of steam once they crack the top ten? Can they become the top-ranked player in the world, even if for a week? Will they go on to become one of the best ever?

It is difficult to tell, and back in 1999, these were the kinds of questions swirling around Serena Williams. If you are a tennis fan, then you likely know how the story ends, but at this point, Serena was only 17 years old. Though she was heading into the 1999 US Open as the seventh seed, her career had not yet blossomed.

She entered the tournament without ever having advanced past the fourth round of any tournament, and while Serena believed that she could play well, she wasn't expecting to win.

She opened the tournament against Tatiana Poutchek, a Belarusian qualifier, whom Williams dispatched 6-1, 6-2. It was an easy opening round, but she needed a few extra games to defeat Anne-Gaelle Sidot of France. Williams won in straight sets, 6-4, 6-3.

Then, a lucky break came for Williams when her slated opponent for the third round had to withdraw, leaving Williams with a free pass to the fourth round.

The rest may have contributed to Williams' slow start in her next match, leaving her down one set to MJ Fernandez of the United States. However, Williams found her stride, and after losing the first set, she rallied to win the second and third sets. A 2-6, 6-1, 6-0 victory sent Williams to the quarterfinals, where she had to face Monica Seles.

At this point, Seles was the fourth seed, meaning that Williams' competition would be much tougher moving forward. This was evident in the first set, which Seles took by a 6-4 margin. Despite being in uncharted territory, Williams was not intimidated by her first quarter-final appearance. She rallied, using her power to overwhelm Seles and win the match, 4-6, 6-3, 6-2.

Adding to all of this was the success Serena's sister, Venus, was having. Venus was also a winner in the quarterfinals, meaning half of the competitors in the semifinals were the Williams sisters! It must have been tough to compete at the highest level of tennis with the pressure of your sister being one of the competitors.

Still, Serena had to prepare for Lindsay Davenport, the second-seeded player in the tournament. Determined to have a stronger start than her previous two rounds, Williams took the first set, 6-4. Davenport was a strong player, though, and she dominated the second set, 6-1. However, Serena was ready to show her mettle at the top of the tennis world. She took the final set, 6-4. It was off to the US Open Final for her.

In the final match of the tournament, Williams faced Martina Hingis, the top-ranked player. Williams continued her fantastic run, winning the first set, 6-3. The second set was a closer contest, going to a tiebreak.

Williams won the tiebreak, 7-4, winning the set, 7-6, and capturing her first major championship. She went on to win 22 more during her amazing career, and it all began with that one big breakthrough.

# Arthur Ashe Paves the Path in the USA

Arthur Ashe Stadium is the main arena for the US Open tournament, so you have likely heard his name before. However, you may not know his story and how much he contributed to the sport of tennis.

Ashe grew up in the United States during the period of segregation, when non-White people were not allowed to use the same facilities as White people. It often meant that Black people were given fewer resources and opportunities to be successful. Young Black people like Arthur Ashe had to work much harder to find success.

Ashe wanted to play football as a kid, but his father refused to allow it. Instead, Arthur settled on tennis. He had a stroke of luck when a local coach named Ron Charity saw Arthur's talent and helped coach and guide him. It also helped that Arthur lived with his father on the grounds of a local park, giving him access to the tennis court.

In 1958, due to his hard work, Ashe became the first Black player to compete in the Maryland boys' championships. It was also Ashe's first time playing in an integrated tournament. While it was a big step forward, the progress did not last. Ashe would not compete against White players again for a couple of years, though his skill was undeniable.

He was the first Black player to win the National Junior Indoor Tennis Championship, and he was featured in *Sports Illustrated* during his rise in the rankings. In 1963, Ashe made history once again by becoming the first Black player selected to the United States Davis Cup team.

In 1968, Ashe won the US Open, which was also the first year of the Open Era, meaning that he could financially benefit from his tennis career. Ashe went on to win the Australian Open in 1970, and he would capture a Wimbledon championship in 1975. He helped the US team earn four Davis Cup championships in 1963, 1968, 1969, and 1970.

He was inducted into the International Tennis Hall of Fame in 1985.

Although his highest-ever ranking was second, which he achieved in 1976, Arthur Ashe's career is remembered more for his contribution to the game, and how his skill and perseverance overcame the racism and discrimination that plagued the United States at the time.

He also worked tirelessly to help tennis players secure their rights against promoters and associations, and he served as the president of the Association of Tennis Professionals during his career.

Tragically, Ashe passed away at the age of 49 from AIDS-related pneumonia. His funeral was held at the Athletic Center named after him, in Richmond, Virginia. More than 5,000 people attended the funeral to celebrate his contributions to tennis and the world.

Arthur Ashe was the first Black man to win Wimbledon, and though the color barrier is not something that exists in many areas of the world today, it was a substantial hurdle for many. His bravery and dedication to the sport of tennis, and to his fellow human beings, remain unmatched to this day.

# Esther Vergeer's Wheelchair Tennis Dominance

Living with a disability can often be a difficult, draining experience. Whether it is physical or mental, anything that takes extra energy to manage can take away from other areas of your life where it may be needed.

It can be too much to overcome, in some cases. Others find a way to persevere. They make a difference where they can. Esther Vergeer is an example of one such individual who sought to achieve greatness despite her physical limitations.

At six years old, Esther began experiencing fluid buildup in her brain. Two years later, she began to experience more symptoms that ultimately resulted in a stroke. An abnormal blood supply around her spinal cord was the culprit. A long surgery alleviated the issue, but the procedure left her unable to use her legs.

Unwilling to give up her passion for sports, Esther began learning to play basketball, tennis, and volleyball. She found great success in basketball, even winning a European championship with the Dutch national team in 1996. However, she also began to experience success on the tennis court.

Within two years, Esther was part of the top-ranked doubles team, and her top ranking in singles followed a few months later, in April 1999. What followed was an incredible winning streak that few would have even considered possible.

Starting in 2001, and moving forward over the next 12 years, Esther Vergeer participated in 560 singles matches. Of those 560 matches, Vergeer won 559 of them. She lost once in 2003, but there were no other blemishes on her record.

Even more impressive was that she was dominant within those matches. She gathered a streak of 250 straight set wins. Of those

250 sets, only one required a tiebreaker. That means that she won more than 120 matches in straight sets! It was a powerful streak of play from a player who seemingly could not lose.

Vergeer retired from professional tennis in 2013, ending her career with 21 Grand Slam titles to her name. She also collected three gold medals in the Paralympics, winning in 2004, 2008, and 2012.

She also used her passion for sports to bring more opportunities to children with disabilities. The Esther Vergeer Foundation began in 2004, working to give kids with disabilities the chance to play games and sports.

Esther Vergeer was a dominant force in the world of wheelchair tennis, and her passion for sports extended to her foundation, giving more children the same opportunities she had. Though she did not have the fame and attention of tennis players like the Williams sisters, news outlets and big tennis stars noticed her accomplishments and paid her the respect she deserved.

In total, she won 96.6% of her singles matches and 92.6% of her doubles matches. It was a run of dominance that will likely never be matched in any sport.

# A Tennis Quiz

1.  The men's Wimbledon trophy has what kind of fruit displayed on its top?

    A. Apple
    B. Pineapple
    C. Grapes
    D. Oranges

2.  The original tennis balls were not yellow. Instead, which color were they?

    A. Black or white
    B. Blue or red
    C. Red or white
    D. Black or red

3.  The record-long match between Isner and Mahut was played over how many days?

    A. One
    B. Two
    C. Three
    D. Four

4.  How quick was the fastest serve ever recorded?

    A. 253.1 km/h
    B. 255.7 km/h
    C. 263 km/h
    D. 259 km/h

5.  Tennis was not played in the Olympics for how many years after 1924?

    A. 32

B. 52

C. C. 56D. 64

6. **Chris Evert holds the record with 125 consecutive match victories on which surface?**

    A. Grass

    B. Clay

    C. Hard

    D. Carpet

7. **Which king's love of tennis contributed to his assassination in the 1400s?**

    A. James I of Scotland

    B. King James II

    C. Henry V

    D. Edward IV

8. **Which top men's player has won more French Opens than any other?**

    A. Novak Djokovic

    B. Rafael Nadal

    C. Roger Federer

    D. Pete Sampras

9. **Which women's player has more Open Era Wimbledon titles than any other?**

    A. Martina Navratilova

    B. Steffi Graf

    C. Serena Williams

    D. Billie Jean King

10. **Andre Agassi famously learned to read which great tennis player by looking at his tongue during serves?**

A. Pete Sampras
B. Roger Federer
C. John McEnroe
D. Bjorn Borg

# CHAPTER 3
# BOXING AND MIXED MARTIAL ARTS

# A Brief History of Combat Sports

Combat sports have been around since ancient times, with evidence of sports similar to boxing and wrestling in places like China, Japan, Egypt, and India. The ancient Olympic Games also had many combat sports, including pankration, which was similar to mixed martial arts as it was a grappling and striking combat sport with no weapons.

The Middle Ages and Renaissance periods also saw tournaments become popular. These events often featured many forms of combat sports. Boxing, or prizefighting, developed into modern boxing when the Marquess of Queensbury rules were introduced in 1867, and amateur boxing has been a staple of the modern Olympic Games since 1904. As it grew in popularity, other combat sports around the world began to spread and evolve.

While combat sports dipped in popularity after World War I, a related form grew in popularity, known as show' wrestling. This was the early precursor to such entertainment companies as World Wrestling Entertainment and All Elite Wrestling, which focus on storytelling, performance, and drama.

Meanwhile, when martial arts from Asian countries reached Brazil, they morphed into Brazilian Jiu-Jitsu. Muay Thai as it is known today was developed in the 1920s and 30s. Sambo became popular in the Soviet Union around the same time, while Taekwondo developed during the 1940s and 50s.

All of these fighting styles developing at the same time led to the concept of mixed martial arts. As unrestricted fights between the different styles grew in popularity, so did the idea of the Ultimate Fighting Championship.

Another precursor to the idea behind mixed martial arts is, strangely enough, thanks in part to one of the best boxers of all time, Muhammad Ali. He fought in a 1976 exhibition bout against wrestler Antonio Inoki in Japan. This helped develop the idea of the Pride Fighting Championships, another production company for mixed martial arts competitions.

The Ultimate Fighting Championship, which began in 1993, sought to test the idea of which fighting style was king in a one-on-one contest, and it quickly captured attention in the United States before spreading around the world. It has since developed into one of the most popular combat sport production companies in human history.

It has brought more eyes to the sport and helped athletes fight in a variety of different ways. Between mixed martial arts and the popularity of boxing in much of the world, combat sports have continued to grow in popularity.

Boxing has also enjoyed a great deal of popularity in the last 30 years thanks to some fantastic performances from names such as Mike Tyson, Floyd Mayweather, and Tyson Fury.

It is quite clear that combat sports are only becoming more popular, and this trend will likely continue as the internet helps viewers see more of the contests they care about.

# Fun Combat Sports Facts

1. Boxing first appeared as an Olympic event during the 23rd Olympiad, which took place in 688 BCE.
2. *Vale tudo*, which translates to "anything goes" from Portuguese to English, was a form of "no holds barred" fighting that became very popular in Brazil beginning in the 1920s.
3. The Unified Rules of Mixed Martial Arts were developed and rolled out in 2000, which coincided with an uptick in popularity for the sport.
4. The first form of wrestling to debut at the modern Olympics was the Greco-Roman style, which does not allow any holds below the waist.
5. Bare-knuckle boxing was popular for the first half of the 18th century in England, until fixed fights became too common, pushing spectators away from the sport.
6. Almost half of Floyd Mayweather's 50 wins came against boxers who were also champions at the time they faced Mayweather. He defeated 23 champions.
7. Muhammad Ali is the only boxer to be an undisputed heavyweight champion on three different occasions.
8. As of 2024, Khabib Nurmagomedov is the only UFC fighter to have a perfect record with more than ten fights under his belt.
9. Anderson Silva holds the distinction of winning 16 straight UFC matches, an unmatched record in the organization.
10. As of May 11, 2024, Charles Oliveira has collected 20 finishes throughout his career, more than any other UFC fighter.

# Great Combat Sports Stories

## Rumble in the Jungle

Few fights in boxing history have as much history and excitement behind them as the Rumble in the Jungle, from 1974. It was a special, one-of-a-kind event between two amazing boxers, in a location not typically used for boxing events. These details, coupled with extra effort added to televise the event, created one of the biggest moments in boxing history.

In one corner was George Foreman, the undisputed heavyweight champion with a gaudy 40-0 record, 37 of those wins by knockout. At the time of the fight, he was 25 years old and at the top of his game. He had won a gold medal at the 1968 Olympics and many people favored him to win the bout against his older opponent.

The opponent, though, was former heavyweight champion Muhammad Ali. Back in 1967, Ali had been stripped of his title for refusing to comply with the military draft in the United States. Then, as he climbed back up the ranks, he lost to Joe Frazier, the champion at the time, sending Ali back down the ranks.

This fight represented Ali's rise as a top contender once more, but at 32 years of age, many could not fathom any way he would be able to survive Foreman's attack.

The fight took place in Zaire, which is now known as the Democratic Republic of the Congo. The two fighters spent months in the area, acclimating to the humidity and training for the fight.

People around the world were enthralled. Some estimates neared one billion viewers between pay-per-view buys and closed-circuit theater television.

The fight was just as epic as billed, though the outcome involved a revolutionary new style of defense for the sport.

While the first round saw both fighters on the attack, the second round went differently. Ali, looking to avoid many of the power punches to come from Foreman, began to cover up and lean against the ropes, increasing the distance between the two fighters.

As Ali leaned away from his opponent, Foreman continued to throw punches that landed without much effect. Ali would counter with quick jabs and crosses when possible, and this is how the fight continued for several rounds. Foreman began to tire, and the two boxers continued to trade blows until the eighth round.

As Foreman's attack began to weaken from fatigue, Ali pounced on the opportunity. With several hooks over Foreman's slowing jab, then a five-punch combination ending in a left hook that sent Foreman's chin up, Ali finished the attack with a hard right-hand square to the face, sending Foreman to the canvas.

The defending champion tried to regain his footing, but the referee signaled the end of the fight before Foreman could recover. It was an incredible finish to a fantastic fight on a spectacular worldwide stage. Both fighters were praised for their performances, and the world was shocked by Muhammad Ali's return to the top of the sport after so many years away.

This fight, along with a few others, cemented Ali's legacy as one of the best boxers to ever step into the ring. After all, few others have introduced new strategies and revolutionized the sport as Ali did.

# Mayweather vs. Pacquiao

When it comes to welterweight fighters, few can argue the greatness that was both Floyd Mayweather and Manny Pacquiao in the 2000s and 2010s. The two fighters both held title belts, and the two were throwing barbs against each other as early as 2009, but the camps could not make a deal to get a fight on the books.

Fast forward to May 2015, and the stage was finally set to settle the score between these two greats. Mayweather was coming into the fight undefeated, with 47 wins, 27 by knockout. He was known for his amazing defensive skills and quick counterpunches. He held three title belts and was considered the top-ranked pound-for-pound fighter at the time.

Manny Pacquiao came to the fight with one championship belt, and a record of 57 wins, five losses, and two draws. He had 38 knockouts to his name, a statistic that represented the speed and power of his offensive skills.

Adding more fire to the fight was the fact that Mayweather had canceled an earlier retirement decision from years prior. As Pacquiao threatened to overshadow Mayweather's boxing resume, Floyd returned to continue and keep the possibility of a showdown on the table.

Fans had waited for years, so when the fight finally arrived, many were disappointed by what happened in the ring.

It became clear that Mayweather was going to rely on defense to win the contest. He consistently covered up and leaned against the ropes, just as Ali had so many years ago. However, fans were not appreciative of this strategy. They wanted to see more action, even though both boxers were landing punches.

Throughout the fight, Mayweather continued to defend, landing counterpunches when possible as Pacquiao did his best to inflict damage without tiring himself out. The two boxers continued in this fashion for much of the fight until the final round. Pacquiao continued to chase Mayweather around the ring, trying desperately to land the big punch that could win the fight. Mayweather continued his countering and even raised his hand in victory as the final seconds ticked off the clock.

All three judges gave the fight to Floyd Mayweather, preserving his undefeated record and making him the undisputed champion as his career cruised toward its end. He fought two more times, defeating Andre Berto by unanimous decision, then winning a fight against MMA fighter Conor McGregor, by TKO in the tenth round of 12. His final fight occurred at age 40.

Manny Pacquiao fought seven more times before retiring in 2021, winning five and losing two. He defeated Timothy Bradley, Jessie Vargas, Lucas Matthysse, Adrien Broner, and Keith Thurman. His losses came against Jeff Horn and Yordenis Ugas. By the time Pacquiao was done with fighting, he was 42 years old.

Both fighters will be remembered in boxing history for their greatness - even if their clash wasn't the blockbuster fight everyone wanted it to be. Boxing can be about defense, too.

# Tyson Captivates and Crashes

In terms of meteoric boxing rises, few have captivated the world as quickly and as effectively as Mike Tyson. As a young boxer, Tyson learned from some great trainers, such as Kevin Rooney and Teddy Atlas.

His professional career began in 1985, and in his first year as a professional, he fought 15 times. In his first 28 professional fights, he had 26 knockouts. Of those 26 knockouts, 16 of them took place in the first round. He was winning fights with pure explosiveness, blitzing opponents with power punches before the fight could even begin.

Sure, Tyson fought a lot of journeymen to start his career, but the quality of his opponents quickly increased as he sought to improve his standing in the boxing rankings. However, some wondered if his rise up the rankings and fame across the country would affect the young man, who had had a troubled childhood.

After all, when a person's life changes drastically, it can be difficult to adjust.

In November 1986, not even two years after his professional career began, Mike Tyson was in a title fight against Trevor Berbick for the World Boxing Council (WBC) heavyweight championship.

You can likely guess what happened next. Mike Tyson won the title with a second-round TKO, becoming the youngest heavyweight champion in history!

In 1987, he added two more belts to his collection. His duck-and-weave defense coupled with the explosive power of his punches could not be overcome. He was a boxing sensation, captivating the country. Video game maker, Nintendo, even approached Tyson about putting him into a boxing game.

However, as he continued to gain fame, his personal troubles began to catch up with him. He had a close call against Frank Bruno, who stunned Tyson early, though Tyson recovered to win by knockout in the fifth round. Then, in February 1990, Tyson lost to Buster Douglas, a fighter Tyson was favored to defeat by odds of 42/1.

It was only a taste of things to come. Mike Tyson won more big fights, but he was arrested and imprisoned in February 1992, not being released until 1995.

Then, in November 1996, Mike Tyson lost to Evander Holyfield.

Seven months later, there was a rematch. However, that fight never finished. Mike Tyson was disqualified for biting off a chunk of Holyfield's ear! It was a moment that many consider to be one of the most shocking in professional boxing history.

From there, Tyson was widely considered to be done in terms of professional fights. He would have a few more big fights, including a title fight against Lennox Lewis, but he was knocked out in the eighth round of that fight.

Mike Tyson's boxing career started strong, and many people consider him one of the greatest fighters of the time. However, we are left wondering what could have been. If Mike Tyson had the guidance to be successful, he may have been the greatest heavyweight champion of all time.

# Jon Jones' Troubled Reign

In the world of mixed martial arts, it is rare to get through a career without losing. For some, it is also difficult to avoid controversy.

Jon Jones is considered one of the greatest MMA fighters in UFC history despite several controversial moments that have stained his career.

It began quickly for Jones, who found himself rapidly moving up the UFC rankings at a very young age. He started his career with a win by unanimous decision over Andre Gusmao at UFC 87 in August 2008. Jones accepted the fight on short notice, too, making the beginning of his rise even more sudden.

Another win against the big and physical Stephan Bonnar at UFC 94 gained Jones more attention, especially for his big suplexes and back elbow attacks that were underused by other fighters.

His third fight was another victory, this time by guillotine choke. Jones had won three fights in less than a year, and he had the attention of the UFC.

Five months later, though, Jones would get into his first bit of trouble. In a fight against Matt Hamill, Jones was disqualified for illegal downward elbow strikes. The UFC has tried to get the fight result changed to a No Contest, but the Nevada State Athletic Commission has not changed it. The loss for Jones would stain his record permanently, though many do not consider it a loss.

Still, Jones continued pushing forward. In his next fight, he broke Brandon Vera's face in three places and won by TKO, then defeated Vladimir Matyushenko by TKO with elbows in the first round.

In February 2011, Jones defeated Ryan Bader, then earned a title shot one month later.

In March 2011, Jones became the youngest-ever UFC champion by defeating Mauricio Rua by TKO.

Jones successfully defended his belt against Quinton Jackson, Lyoto Machida, and Rashad Evans before defeating Vitor Belfort. It was a string of title defenses rarely seen in UFC history, further cementing Jones' legacy.

In May 2015, though, Jones was suspended after being connected to a traffic incident. His belt was stripped, and he would have to get it back. However, he was suspended again in 2016 for an illegal drug found in his system. This would reoccur in July 2017, again stripping the belt from Jones and further staining his legacy.

Despite the controversies, Jones has continued to compete in the UFC, winning the Light Heavyweight Championship against Alexander Gustafsson, and then defending it against Anthony Smith.

Jones had another close call when he needed a split decision to escape a challenge from Thiago Santos. Finally, he defeated Dominick Reyes by unanimous decision before vacating the Light Heavyweight belt.

Three years later, Jones challenged Ciryl Gane for the Heavyweight Championship. Just two minutes into the first round, Jones submitted Gane by a guillotine choke, earning him another belt in the UFC.

While Jones continues to achieve successes in the octagon, his struggles outside of it also persist. What his final story will be, anyone can guess. In the meantime, fans will continue to enjoy the power and skill Jones demonstrates in his fights. After all, that is how the UFC finds success. The best fighters bring the crowds, and Jon Jones is one of the very best.

# Anderson Silva

Anderson "The Spider" Silva is widely regarded as one of the most skilled MMA fighters in the sport's history. His time with the UFC demonstrated his ability to finish fights in some of the most incredible fashions, and his time with the championship belt is one of the most dominant runs ever.

Growing up in poverty, Anderson began training in jiu-jitsu with other neighborhood kids in Curitiba, Brazil. He would go on to receive training in muay thai, capoeira, and taekwondo, making his training very well-rounded.

His path to the UFC was a long one, though. He began his professional career back in 1997, going 11-1 in his first 12 fights. He then traveled to Japan and became the first person to defeat the 20-0 Hayato Sakurai to become the new Shooto Middleweight Champion.

From there, Silva found his way to Pride Fighting Championships. After several victories, Silva was defeated in a surprise upset by Daiju Takase. The defeat caused Silva to consider quitting MMA, but he persisted and continued to find victories.

In 2006, Silva finally landed with the UFC, and he didn't wait long to make his mark on the new company. His first opponent, Chris Leben, said he would knock out Silva. Instead, Silva only needed 49 seconds to knock out Leben with 85% striking accuracy.

This emphatic victory earned Silva a title shot against Middleweight Champion Rich Franklin. Another TKO victory made Silva the new champion, and what followed was incredible and record-breaking.

He defended his title ten times, defeating some of the biggest names in the UFC along the way, often in impressive fashion. However, there were signs that Silva was losing sight of the discipline that had brought him so far in his career. In his fight against Demian Maia, he spent much of the fight circling and taunting his opponent, disappointing the UFC managers and fans along the way.

Then, though he had decided to retire after defeating Stephan Bonnar in the first round, he agreed to fight Chris Weidman and defend his belt once more.

In that fight, Silva was too busy showboating to see the threat that Weidman posed. Silva was knocked out in the second round, ending his record reign as champion.

Then, in the rematch, Silva's leg broke horribly, ending the fight and Silva's dominance in the UFC. To his credit, he continued to fight after his recovery, even defeating Nick Diaz by decision in 2015. Then, it was revealed that Silva failed drug tests surrounding the fight, further tainting Silva's legacy with the UFC.

Silva fought with the UFC until 2020, when he was released from his contract.

Though his career was not perfect, and he ultimately fell to his own pride and hubris, Anderson Silva was one of the most entertaining and dominant champions in UFC history. His victories brought people to their feet, and he will always be remembered for those moments.

# The Thrilla in Manila

In boxing history, there have been some great matches and some even better rematches. Few rivalries have reached the ultimate trilogy of contests. After all, it is rare that two boxers at the top of their game need multiple opportunities to prove who is the best.

One of those boxers, Muhammad Ali, was coming into the fight with a 48-2 record, including 34 knockouts. Joe Frazier, his opponent, came into the fight with a 32-2 record, with 27 knockouts.

But, before we get to the fight, we should quickly recap what happened in the first two matches. The first showdown between these two titans of boxing was dubbed the "Fight of the Century." Frazier was the champion coming into the fight, and he was the champion walking out of it, as he defeated Ali by unanimous decision. The only knockdown of that fight occurred at the beginning of the 15th round, which Frazier scored against Ali.

Almost three years later, neither contender was a champion for their rematch. Although there was some controversy with the refereeing, Ali came away with the decision victory.

Another year and a half later, the two boxers were ready to settle the score once and for all. This time, Ali was the one entering the bout as champion, having defeated George Foreman in Zaire.

This fight, as you can tell by the title, was held in the Philippines. Just like the Rumble in the Jungle, it is estimated that a billion people were tuned in to the fight, ready to see which of these two giants would come out on top.

Ali was quick on his feet, looking for counterattacks while Frazier liked to hit hard and punish his opponents. It was a contrast in style, very similar to the fight that Ali had won against Foreman a couple of years before.

When the fight began, Ali was the faster starter, winning the first two rounds with quick jabs and moving feet. Frazier found himself knocked off balance twice in the first few rounds, and he also found himself subject to more of Ali's famous taunts during the fight.

As the two continued to battle, Frazier focused on body blows to take some of the energy away from Ali, while the champ used countering jabs and crosses as he continued to defend. As the fight progressed, though, Frazier began to get the better of Ali, as Joe had learned the rhythm of Ali's movements.

This momentum came to a crescendo in the sixth round, when Frazier landed two incredible shots to Ali's face and upper body.

When Ali didn't go down, though, Frazier had to wonder if there was anything he could do. The swelling began to creep into Frazier's face, nearly shutting his eyes. Ali took advantage and punished his opponent in the 13th and 14th rounds, causing Frazier's trainer to throw in the towel before the final round.

Ali would later confess that he was moments away from throwing in the towel himself.

The two men had pushed each other to the limit, making boxing history in the process.

# A Boxing and MMA Quiz

1. Who is the only heavyweight boxing champion to retire undefeated?

   A. Rocky Marciano
   B. Lennox Lewis
   C. Larry Holmes
   D. Wladimir Klitschko

2. Which boxing legend had a Detroit, Michigan arena named after him?

   A. Rocky Marciano
   B. Joe Louis
   C. Max Schmeling
   D. Jack Dempsey

3. Which boxer was the oldest to ever win a world championship?

   A. George Foreman
   B. Muhammad Ali
   C. Floyd Mayweather
   D. Bernard Hopkins

4. Which of these boxers was known as "The Golden Boy"?

   A. Oscar De La Hoya
   B. Evander Holyfield
   C. Floyd Mayweather
   D. Muhammad Ali

5. Muhammad Ali's daughter, Laila, boxed professionally to an undefeated record. How many matches did she win before retiring?

A. 21

B. 22

C. 23

D. 24

6. Which UFC fighter has competed in more title bouts than any other?

   A. Jon Jones

   B. Randy Couture

   C. Georges St-Pierre

   D. Demetrious Johnson

7. As of UFC 300, which UFC fighter has more fight victories than any other competitor?

   A. Andrei Arlovski

   B. Donald Cerrone

   C. Dustin Poirier

   D. Jim Miller

8. Which competitor has the most finishes in title fights, always wanting to put on a show for the crowd?

   A. Ronda Rousey

   B. Matt Hughes

   C. Anderson Silva

   D. Demetrious Johnson

9. Which UFC fighter holds the record for the fastest finish in a title bout?

   A. Ronda Rousey

   B. Andrei Arlovski

   C. Frank Shamrock

   D. Conor McGregor

10. Which fighter is the only UFC competitor to finish a title bout with one second left on the clock?

    A. Ronda Rousey
    B. Matt Hughes
    C. Anderson Silva
    D. Demetrious Johnson

# CHAPTER 4
# ICE HOCKEY

# A Brief History of Ice Hockey

Ice hockey's origins are difficult to trace directly, as several kinds of similar stick-and-ball sports were imported to North America from various countries around the world. Many historians believe the sport evolved from games such as bandy, shinty, hurling, and even lacrosse.

As field hockey in England was just called hockey back in the 1700s, inventors of the new game simply added the word "ice" to distinguish their game from its similar predecessor. It is also believed that the word "puck" is derived from the Scottish Gaelic "puc," or the similar Irish word "poc," both of which have a similar meaning: to deliver a blow, or to poke.

From there, the game evolved and organizing began in the city of Montreal, Quebec, Canada. The first organized game of ice hockey played indoors took place in March 1875 between students from McGill University. Even at this very first organized game, there are records indicating that the spectators were surprised by the violent nature of the contest.

Still, the game continued to grow in popularity, and McGill was again early to the party, as they created the first ice hockey club in 1877. As more teams came into existence, competition began to spread. In 1883, the first "world championship" tournament took place in Montreal. Of course, McGill won.

Three years later, the Amateur Hockey Association of Canada was formed, which began the tradition of seasonal play every year. As hockey continued to grow, fans of the sport began contributing. One such fan, Lord Stanley of Preston, realized that there was no trophy to recognize the best team in Canada. He purchased a silver bowl that he named the Dominion Hockey Challenge Cup, and it was first awarded in 1893.

From there, professional leagues sprouted up everywhere, leading to the condensing of competition. The National Hockey Association was formed in 1910, based in Montreal. That league helped further refine the rules of the game, many of which are still in use today. Seven years later, that league expanded and renamed itself to the National Hockey League.

In 1924, the National Hockey League crossed Canada's southern border by adding the Boston Bruins to the league.

While leagues in Canada and the United States were continuing to grow, leagues were also sprouting up in countries such as Russia, Czechoslovakia, Finland, and Sweden. Of those leagues, Switzerland is credited with being one of the first, forming their National League A in 1916, only a few years after the National Hockey Association.

From there, the game has continued to evolve. Rule changes have forced players and coaches to adjust their approaches to success, and the game has continuously gotten faster and more skilled every year.

It is still a violent game at times, but it is nothing like it once was. Even in the last 30 years with the removal of "enforcers," the game has moved toward skill and speed, leaving behind the grabbing and checking of the past.

# Fun Ice Hockey Facts

1. Hockey pucks are kept frozen before use in games, as they tend to become very bouncy if they are warm.
2. The Stanley Cup, awarded to the NHL champion every year, weighs 37 pounds and is 35.25 inches tall.
3. During the 1974 Draft, the Buffalo Sabres made up a fictional player to draft in the 11th round. It was their way of protesting the slow process that was the NHL Draft.
4. Hockey goals are four feet tall and six feet wide, and the goal line is two inches wide.
5. Ice hockey is the only major sport that allows substitutions during live play. It does not require a stop in play for players to switch with teammates on the bench.
6. Canada and the United States are the only two countries that have won the women's Ice Hockey World Championship.
7. The Montreal Canadiens have more Stanley Cup victories than any other team in the NHL.
8. Bobby Orr of the Boston Bruins was the first NHL player awarded with a contract worth $1 million, though it was paid out over five years.
9. The oldest player to play in the NHL was Gordie Howe, at 52 years and 11 days old.
10. Wayne Gretzky won the NHL MVP award eight seasons in a row, an untouchable record.

# Great Ice Hockey Stories

## Lemieux's Return

Mario Lemieux played his entire NHL career with the Pittsburgh Penguins, and during his time with the organization, he delivered some great moments on and off the ice. He served as the team's captain for most of those years with the team, and he put everything he had into making the team better.

He was one of the best players in the league at the time, and many consider him to be one of the best players in the history of the game. He often competed with Wayne Gretzky for scoring titles, and he helped his team win championships.

When a player cares that much about his team, the city, and the fans, then the fans will rally around that player. Well, there came a time in Lemieux's career when he needed that support.

During the 1992–93 NHL season, "Super" Mario noticed that a lump on his neck, which had been there for over a year, was starting to get larger. He brought it to the attention of the team's doctor, who had Mario get it removed by specialists. When it was tested, the doctors discovered that Lemieux had Hodgkin's Lymphoma.

Mario Lemieux missed several games to receive 22 treatments, but on the day of his final treatment, March 2, 1993, Lemieux decided he was ready to get back on the ice. It just so happened that his team was playing in Philadelphia that evening, against their rivals, the Flyers. Lemieux booked a private flight to Philadelphia in time to start the game, despite not having practiced in two months.

It was an emotional moment for him, but few could guess what would happen when he stepped onto the ice. The fans in Philadelphia, typically rowdy and very hostile to the Penguins, stood up and cheered for Lemieux and his return to the ice.

It was a moment of humanity that will give chills to any hockey fan.

The fans in Philadelphia did not cheer much when Lemieux scored his 40th goal of the year in the second period of that game, though.

Mario Lemieux had faced cancer and won, and he returned to hockey as soon as he could. Incredibly, Lemieux managed to collect 160 points on the season, winning the NHL scoring record in 1993. He scored more points than any other player even though he had missed two months of the season!

It was an incredible individual performance, and it showed how much Lemieux loved the game of hockey.

Mario Lemieux would go on to enter the Hockey Hall of Fame in 1997, and he continued to play for the Penguins from 2000 to 2006, even though he owned part of the team. Yes, you read that right. In case he hadn't already done enough for the team and the city of Pittsburgh, he helped purchase some of the team's shares so it wouldn't move to another city.

He literally saved the city, and perhaps the spirit of the city - just as the team's fans had helped to save him when he needed it.

## Paul Kariya Gets Up

Ice hockey is well known for the violence that sometimes plays out on the ice. Players are looking to hit others when possible, even if the puck has moved away. Big hits can change the outlook of a game, giving momentum to the more aggressive team as they look to assert their dominance on the ice.

Sometimes, though, a player can overcome a massive hit and make a difference on the ice for their team. One example of this kind of play took place during the 2003 Stanley Cup Finals as the New Jersey Devils faced the Mighty Ducks of Anaheim.

The two players that figured in the big play were Scott Stevens, a big defenseman known for throwing punishing open-ice hits against his opponents, and Paul Kariya, a skilled player known for his goalscoring and playmaking abilities in the offensive zone.

It is Game 6 of the Finals. The Devils are one victory away from the Stanley Cup, but the game is in Anaheim, and the hosting Mighty Ducks have a 3-1 lead nearing the halfway point of the second period.

Anaheim's Paul Kariya intercepts a neutral zone pass and turns up ice, skating toward the Devils' zone. He makes a backhand pass to a teammate skating up the boards, but instead of looking around and seeing where to skate next, Kariya's eyes never leave the puck.

The Devils' Scott Stevens is coming from the other side of the ice, and Kariya never sees him coming.

The hit is thunderous, and Kariya is sent down to the ice, hard. Lying flat on his back, he slides a couple of feet before coming to a stop, and he is not moving.

The arena explodes in anger before going silent. Kariya is met by a trainer, who starts trying to figure out the situation. Then, while a TV camera has zoomed in on Kariya's face, fans watching at home breathe a sigh of relief when they see Kariya's face shield suddenly fog up as he breathes out, returning to consciousness.

He gets up on his own, but his teammates help him off the ice and into the locker room.

After a hit like that, players are usually done for the game, maybe the series.

Paul Kariya is not done. With about four minutes left in the second period, he returns to the bench. The crowd sees him and cheers in approval.

Then, he gives them another reason to cheer. On his next shift, he gets the puck and races up the ice, releasing a slapshot that beats Devils goalie Martin Brodeur over the glove and into the net, sending the crowd into a frenzy.

It was an incredible moment in the series.

The Ducks would win Game 6, forcing a Game 7 in New Jersey, where they would lose to the Devils.

Although the series did not have the storybook ending after the incredible chapter that was Game 6, Paul Kariya's bravery and determination will live on as one of the best moments in hockey history.

## Gordie Howe's Long Career

A long career in today's NHL is around 20 years. If a player has that long a career without any substantial injuries, it is considered a great success. It is no wonder, then, that one special hockey player made such an impact on the league and the game, as he played the sport for much longer than anyone else.

Gordie Howe is also known as "Mr. Hockey," and it is easy to see why. His hockey career began way back in the 1940s, and his start was a bit earlier than many other players at the time. He was offered a contract at 15 years old when the New York Rangers saw him playing in Canada.

However, he declined that offer and continued playing and practicing in Canada. Then, the Detroit Red Wings came to town. Howe liked that Detroit gave him much easier to access in Canada, and it helped that the Red Wings had a training camp in Windsor, Ontario.

From there, Howe's career skyrocketed. From 1946 to 1980, he played professional hockey for three different teams: the Detroit Red Wings, the Houston Aeros, and the Hartford Whalers.

During those decades of play, Howe collected dozens of awards and records, many of which remain unbroken to this day. He used his physical stature to overpower opponents, and he often resorted to fighting when necessary.

One severe injury threatened to end Howe's young career in 1950, when a check attempt sent him headfirst into the boards, fracturing his skull and leaving his nose and cheekbone broken. He missed the rest of the playoffs that year but returned for the next season. Not only did he return from that terrible injury, but he went on to lead the league in goals and assists. Howe won the scoring title by 20 points that year.

It was a substantial example of Howe's incredible tenacity on the ice, and it was a quality that he never let slip during his time playing the sport. His strength and skill on the ice helped the Red Wings win Stanley Cup Championships in 1950, 1952, 1954, and 1955.

The Detroit Red Wings hold Gordie's time with the team in high reverence, especially because they would have to wait until 1997 to win another championship.

Gordie would leave Detroit in 1971, then play for the Houston Aeros of the World Hockey Association in 1973, scoring 100 points in 70 games during his first year there. In fact, he would continue racking up the points until 1979–80, when he only gathered 41 points in 80 games with the Hartford Whalers of the NHL.

Finally, in 1997, Gordie Howe was invited to play one shift for the International Hockey League's Detroit Vipers, making him the only player to play professional hockey in six different decades.

Gordie Howe still holds several NHL records. He is the only NHL player to score 20 goals in 22 straight seasons. He also holds the record for most games played with a single team, as he played 1,687 games in Detroit. He also holds the distinction of leading the NHL playoffs in scoring six times, more than any other player.

Howe's career was special in many ways, and it is unlikely that anyone will be able to match many of his marks. He was determined to be successful, and not even a fractured skull could stop him.

# The Miracle on Ice

At the 1980 Winter Olympics, few ice hockey teams were expected to compete with the Soviet Union team that had been dominating international hockey for decades. It didn't help that the Soviet squad comprised players that were practically professionals, as they were paid by companies in the country to only play hockey on the international stage.

At this time, though, the Olympics did not allow professional players to compete, so the other teams were comprised of amateur players. The United States team was particularly young, made up of college-level players that averaged 21 years old. It was not looking good for that American team, but they were determined to do their best and make their country proud.

It was a surprise, then, when the Americans escaped the group stage without a loss. They tied the heavily favored Sweden team, then shocked Czechoslovakia with a 7-3 win. It was a big moment against an opponent that many had thought would finish in second place behind the Soviets.

They completed the group stage with victories over Norway, Romania, and West Germany, sending them through to the medal round.

At this point in the tournament, the American squad had already outperformed expectations, so anything else would be frosting on the cake, as they say.

Of course, in the medal round, they faced off against the Soviets. A win would give them a chance to play for a gold medal, but was there even a chance they could win?

Early on in the game, it didn't look like it. Halfway through the first period, Vladimir Krutov scored on a deflection to give the Soviets an early lead. Five minutes later, though, Buzz Schneider connected with a long shot from the boards. The Soviets answered with a little over two minutes left in the period, taking another lead.

However, the Americans would get a lucky bounce when the Soviet keeper Tretiak could not steer away a 100-foot slapshot, leaving the rebound for Mark Johnson to shoot into the goal with only a second on the clock.

It was, somehow, a tie game heading into the second. The Soviets dominated the next frame, but only scored once, taking a 3-2 lead into the third period.

The Americans capitalized on a rare power play opportunity, tying the game at three with a little over ten minutes left in the game. Then, a few moments later, the Americans scored again to take the lead with exactly ten minutes to play.

What followed was some of the most intense, desperate hockey ever played by both teams. For the Soviets, it was a position they rarely found themselves in. For the Americans, the situation required poise and calm, not something for which young teams are renowned.

Still, both teams fought on as the minutes ticked away.

As time wound down, the Soviets' lack of experience trailing cost them, as they never pulled their goaltender. Their coach didn't believe in the practice, and they'd likely had few opportunities to do it before.

The Americans held on to win the game, stunning the hockey world in the process. Fittingly, it was called the "Miracle on Ice."

The American team went on to win the gold, while the Soviets finished in second place because of the round-robin format of the medal round.

# The Red Wings Repeat

The 1997–1998 Detroit Red Wings were coming off a season in which they had won the Stanley Cup for the first time in 42 years. The celebration on the ice and around the city was a great one, but it was short-lived.

News broke that a car accident involving a limousine had injured two Red Wings players and one of the team's trainers. Vladimir Konstantinov, Slava Fetisov, and Sergei Mnatsakanov were all injured in the crash.

Slava Fetisov escaped with comparably minor injuries, but Konstantinov and Mnatsakanov were both severely injured. It was quickly evident that Konstantinov's hockey career was over.

It was a devastating moment for the team, the players, and their families. As they mourned over the summer, it became clear that they would be playing the upcoming season in honor of their injured teammates.

Make no mistake, the Detroit Red Wings were a very good hockey team at this time. However, Konstantinov was a top-pair defenseman, which is a crucial piece of a good hockey team. There would be no way to replace him with anyone nearly as good. Could the team overcome that loss to their roster, not to mention the emotional toll of the tragedy?

The team began the journey, playing games all season with a patch that bore the initials of the two teammates unable to continue in the sport. Slava Fetisov recovered and played that season, helping the team push toward the playoffs.

In the Western Conference, the Red Wings finished the season as the three seed, heading into the playoffs with at least one series with home-ice advantage. They began by defeating the Phoenix Coyotes in six games, earning another home-ice series when Colorado was upset by the Edmonton Oilers.

Next, the Red Wings needed six games once again to defeat the St. Louis Blues. They continued to push forward, needing only eight more wins to win the Cup for Vladdy.

Against Dallas, they won the series in six games once more, and that even included an overtime loss in Game 5 that ended on an error from the Red Wings goaltender, Chris Osgood.

Still, the team knew that Konstantinov and Mnatsakanov and their families were watching. They could not give up!

In the Stanley Cup Finals, they faced the Washington Capitals. In Game 1, they scored twice in the first period and held on to win 2-1. Then in Game 2, they fell behind by multiple goals, even trailing 4-2 in the third period. But a furious comeback and a thrilling overtime goal gave Detroit a 2-0 series lead heading to Washington.

In Game 3, a late goal from superstar Sergei Fedorov gave the Red Wings another win, putting the team one win away from the Cup.

Game 4 was the least contested game. Detroit took a 2-0 lead, and that lead was 3-1 by the end of the second period. Another goal in the third, and the Red Wings were champions again.

When captain Steve Yzerman received the trophy, he lifted it over his head for just a few moments before handing it to Vladimir Konstantinov, who was in his wheelchair on the ice. It was everything the team had worked for all year, and though it couldn't take away the pain, it was healing for all involved.

# Bobby Baun Plays Injured

Anyone familiar with the game of hockey knows that players are well-known for fighting through injuries. Broadcasts will often show players being stitched on the bench, closing cuts as soon as possible to rejoin the action.

One player, Bobby Baun, had a more significant injury during a game in the Stanley Cup Finals, but he found a way to push through. Not only did he insist on playing, but he also made a substantial contribution to his team in the process.

It was 1964, and the Toronto Maple Leafs had reached the Stanley Cup Finals to face the Detroit Red Wings. When the series reached Game 6, though, the Leafs were trailing, facing the end of their season. They needed a win, and going into the third period, each team was pushing for the winning goal in a tied game.

Bobby Baun, a defenseman for the Leafs, was determined to keep his team in the game. Although he was not a scorer, with only three goals in 96 career playoff games, he was a stout defender. Late in the period, with a Red Wings slapshot flying toward the goal, Baun skated into its path.

The puck struck him in the ankle, sending him to the ice in pain. He attempted to skate it off, playing two more short shifts before he heard a popping sound from his ankle. He couldn't put any weight on his leg, leaving him struggling to reach the bench. He ultimately needed a stretcher to get off the ice.

It was a terrible fate for Baun, but when he reached the locker room, he decided that he had more to give. Baun heard that the Leafs had escaped the third period and that the game was headed for overtime. Any hockey player would want to be on the ice for that, and Baun was no exception.

The doctors assigned to the game wanted to send Baun to the hospital, but the team's doctor, Dr. Jim Murray, decided that Baun couldn't do any more damage to his ankle than he already had. So, he had Baun's ankle taped and frozen to numb the pain and sent Baun back to the ice for overtime.

Baun was on the ice for the team's second shift of overtime, and in the offensive zone, as he covered the blue line, the puck came his way. He did his best, while playing on one good leg, to keep the puck in, flinging it weakly toward the Red Wings goal.

Now, any good hockey coach will tell you to put pucks on goal, because you never know what might happen. Well, that advice rang true in this case, as Baun's shot deflected off Red Wings' defenseman Bill Gadsby before making it behind goaltender Terry Sawchuk and into the goal!

Bobby Baun had won the game for the Leafs, keeping their hopes alive for one more game.

It was an incredible moment. But Baun made sure the moment was not for nothing. He refused medical attention and played in Game 7, which the Leafs also won, winning the Stanley Cup. Only when Baun fell while trying to get into a convertible for the team's celebratory parade through the city did he go to the hospital.

He was a dedicated player, as all great hockey players are.

# An Ice Hockey Quiz

1. **Which NHL team has reached the most Stanley Cup Finals?**

   A. Montreal Canadiens
   B. Detroit Red Wings
   C. Toronto Maple Leafs
   D. Boston Bruins

2. **Alex Ovechkin, Wayne Gretzky, and which other NHL player are tied with nine 50-goal seasons?**

   A. Mario Lemieux
   B. Mike Bossy
   C. Guy Lafleur
   D. Marcel Dionne

3. **Which NHL player suited up for 1,779 games over 23 seasons, an NHL record?**

   A. Gordie Howe
   B. Mark Messier
   C. Patrick Marleau
   D. Jaromir Jagr

4. **Which player, as of 2023, has the fastest-ever slapshot on record?**

   A. Zdeno Chara
   B. Filip Hronek
   C. Bobby Hull
   D. Aleksandr Ryazantsev

5. **How many faceoff spots are on a standard hockey rink?**

   A. Six
   B. Seven

C. Eight

D. Nine

6. **How many inches in diameter is the standard hockey puck?**

   A. Two

   B. Three

   C. Four

   D. Five

7. **Who was the first goaltender to wear a mask full-time?**

   A. Terry Sawchuk

   B. Jacques Plante

   C. Glenn Hall

   D. Johnny Bower

8. **What does it mean to put the "biscuit in the basket"?**

   A. Score a goal

   B. Make a great pass

   C. Make a save with the catching glove

   D. Give the puck away

9. **Which NHL team's fans are known for throwing stuffed rats onto the ice in celebration?**

   A. Detroit Red Wings

   B. Seattle Kraken

   C. Florida Panthers

   D. Tampa Bay Lightning

10. **Which NHL team has lost the most Stanley Cup Finals series?**

    A. Montreal Canadiens

    B. Detroit Red Wings

    C. Chicago Blackhawks

    D. Boston Bruins

# CHAPTER 5
# BASKETBALL

# A Brief History of Basketball

The sport of basketball has a solid birthdate in comparison to other popular sports. In December 1891, Dr. James Naismith invented the game when he had to find a way to entertain his college athletes during the winter.

He used peach baskets in his Massachusetts gymnasium and set up his 13 rules for the game. After playing the game with his students, they took the game and began looking for other opponents.

From there the game quickly spread through the colleges and universities in the northeastern United States, along with participation in Canada.

It took a few years to standardize the rules but having five players on each side of the court happened relatively quickly, as that rule came to be in 1895.

The game continued to grow during the early 1900s, and it gained a significant boost in popularity when it was selected as an event for the 1936 Olympics. Like many sports during World War II, basketball suffered, but Naismith's sport saw huge growth when peacetime returned, as countries such as Spain, China, and Italy began to play the sport in larger numbers.

One of the biggest moments for the sport came in 1946 when the National Basketball Association was established in North America. It has become one of the biggest sports leagues in the world, creating world-renowned stars every year.

A key aspect of the modern game, the three-point shot, did not debut in the league until 1979. Once it was introduced, the strategies on the court changed immensely, putting another unique skill on display for others to learn and follow.

The Women's NBA was founded in 1996, and that has helped the sport grow for young women who aspire to play the sport professionally.

Today, the game has influenced popular culture in many regions around the world. It is a sport that has truly grown into a phenomenon.

# Fun Basketball Facts

1.  When basketball was first invented, players were not permitted to dribble. The focus was on passing and moving without the ball.
2.  Dr. Naismith used a soccer ball during the first-ever basketball game, as basketballs did not exist yet.
3.  The official NBA basketball has a circumference of 29.5 inches.
4.  The NBA free throw line is 15 feet away from the backboard.
5.  There is only three feet of space between the corner of the three-point line and the sideline.
6.  Michael Jordan has six championships, but there are nine players throughout league history with more than him.
7.  Wilt Chamberlain is the only NBA player to score 100 points in a single game.
8.  LeBron James is the all-time leading scorer after passing Kareem Abdul-Jabbar.
9.  Muggsy Bogues is the shortest player to ever play in the NBA, at five feet, three inches.
10. The United States defeated Canada 19-8 to win the first-ever Olympic gold in the event, back in 1936.

# Great Basketball Stories

## Magic Johnson Takes Over

It can be a difficult time for a star player when a new, young face joins the team, eager to make his mark. It can be even tougher when that new player just happens to be one of the best in the league.

This was the situation for the Los Angeles Lakers in the 1980 NBA Finals. Magic Johnson was a rookie, having just won the NCAA Championship in 1979 with the Michigan State Spartans. His team defeated Larry Bird and the Indiana State Sycamores.

Johnson was having a great season, but there was one player on his team arguably having a greater one, especially when it came to veteran experience. That was Kareem Abdul-Jabbar, the player who would hold the NBA scoring record until the 2020s.

The team revolved around Kareem and Magic Johnson did well to work with him, leading the Lakers to a strong season. Of course, the players got along well enough to reach the NBA Finals.

Then, Kareem went down with an injury, forcing him out of Game 6. It was an impossible situation for Magic Johnson, in his rookie season, facing the Philadelphia 76ers without his Hall-of-Fame teammate. Even more of a challenge for Johnson was that he would not be able to play point guard with Kareem out. He would play center, taking Kareem's position on the court.

What followed was an incredible piece of NBA history. Johnson scored 42 points, grabbed 15 rebounds, added seven assists, helping the Lakers defeat the 76ers and capture the NBA championship. At the end of the series, Johnson was awarded Finals MVP, and he remains the only rookie in league history to earn that honor.

Over the next several years, Johnson and Abdul-Jabbar would pair up to win four more NBA titles, with some help from James Worthy.

One key moment that demonstrated Kareem's influence on Johnson's game came during Game 4 of the 1987 NBA Finals. Kareem is shooting two free throws very late, and he needs both to tie the game against the Celtics. He makes the first, but the second bounces out, with possession going to the Lakers.

Johnson gets the ball on the inbound pass, but he doesn't pass to an open Kareem. Instead, he dribbles to his right and takes a hook shot, something Kareem was famous for. He makes the shot, the Lakers take a commanding lead in the series, and the basketball world sees the baton passed from one Lakers great to another.

# The Flu Game

Professional athletes have to be in peak physical condition to perform at the highest level of their sport. When they fall ill, it can be a substantial detriment to their abilities. For this reason, players who are sick will often sit out, allowing themselves a chance to recover for the next game. But when it happened in the NBA Finals to one of the best players in league history, the results were completely unbelievable.

Michael Jordan fell ill the night before Game 5 of the 1997 NBA Finals. The series was tied at two games each, and the winner would be one game away from the championship. Some wondered if he had been drinking, or if he had eaten food that was not properly prepared. Either way, the impact was evident in the first quarter, with Jordan looking ineffective.

However, the superstar recovered in the second quarter, scoring 17 points to help keep the game close. It looked like he could take control of the contest at that point, but after halftime, his struggles continued.

His opponents, the Utah Jazz, led by superstars John Stockton and Karl Malone, were doing everything they could to extend their lead, and they had an eight-point lead in the fourth quarter. It looked like the Jazz would take a 3-2 lead in the series, and the Bulls needed their superstar to step up once more. Jordan knew it, so he came back online, scoring seven of Chicago's ten-point run to take the lead in the final minute.

From there, the Bulls were able to hang on for the victory. The famous image from the end of this game was Michael Jordan collapsing into teammate Scottie Pippen's arms, exhausted from the effort and the toll taken on his body. It was an image that showed how much Jordan wanted to win.

They would go on to win Game 6, attaining another championship. At that time, it was Jordan's fifth championship ring and his fifth Finals MVP award.

Michael Jordan and the Bulls would win another championship in 1998, making it six titles in eight years for the dynastic team. Within that impressive era, the Flu Game of 1997 and its contribution to Michael Jordan's legacy loom large in fans' memories.

Many consider him to be the best to ever play the sport, but the Flu Game showed that he had more than talent and moxie on the court. He had an unending determination to be a champion, even when his body was fighting against him.

# Dirk Beats the Big 3

When LeBron James infamously left the Cleveland Cavaliers in search of a team where he could win an NBA championship, many basketball fans around the world expected his new team, the Miami Heat, to win the championship immediately.

After all, he had Chris Bosh and Dwyane Wade on the team, too. Together, the league media dubbed them the "Big 3," and the Heat were the favorites to win simply because of these names on the roster.

At the end of the 2010–2011 regular season, the Heat were the second seed in the East, and they used their veteran experience to roll through the playoffs, reaching the NBA Finals to face Dirk Nowitzki and the Dallas Mavericks. The latter had entered the playoffs as the third seed in the west, just one regular season victory fewer than the Heat.

It was a rematch of the 2006 Finals, when Wade and Shaquille O'Neal defeated Nowitzki to win the championship in six games.

As many expected, Nowitzki led all scorers with 27 points, but the Heat dominated the second half to win Game 1, 92-84.

The first surprise of the series came in Game 2, when the Mavericks stunned the Heat with a 95-93 win, tying the series. They even came back from 15 down in that game.

The teams traded victories in Games 3 and 4, leaving the series tied at two, but Nowitzki was determined to finish the job he had started back in 2006. In Game 5, he exploded for 29 points, leading all scorers once again, helping Dallas to a 112-103 victory.

In Game 6, the Mavericks finished the job, stunning the Heat and the basketball world. Nowitzki won the Finals MVP honors, and LeBron James' quest for an NBA championship was delayed for a year.

LeBron James and the Big 3 would win two championships of their own in the coming years, but few will forget Dirk Nowitzki and the Dallas Mavericks' magical run that seemed to defy the basketball gods at every turn. They delayed the inevitable in Miami and stole a championship at the last possible moment.

While Dirk Nowitzki had a storied NBA career that included being inducted into the Basketball Hall of Fame, his biggest moment will always be his team's triumph over LeBron James, Dwyane Wade, and Chris Bosh, three players also inducted into the Hall of Fame.

# Kobe and Shaq Break Up

Before 2010, it was rare for two of the league's greatest players to be on the same team. But in the late 1990s, the Los Angeles Lakers got lucky. They acquired Shaquille O'Neal, who had started his career with the Orlando Magic, then they drafted a young player named Kobe Bryant, fresh out of high school, in the 1996 NBA Draft.

They didn't know then that Kobe Bryant would go on to be one of hardest working, most talented players in the league's history, but they knew he had the chance to be special. It did not take long for the team to reap the rewards of their new acquisitions.

In Bryant's fourth NBA season, he and O'Neal helped the Lakers win their first NBA championship since 1988. Though there were cracks in the relationship between the two players, including accusations of laziness and missed potential, the duo of superstars combined to win two more NBA championships, making it three in a row for the young all-stars.

O'Neal was convinced that Bryant was a selfish player, and Bryant thought that O'Neal was wasting his potential by not practicing harder and being in better shape. Ultimately, after the 2003–2004 season, in which they lost in the NBA Finals to the Detroit Pistons, O'Neal was traded to the Miami Heat, and Kobe Bryant was re-signed by the Lakers with a huge contract.

The basketball world mourned the tumultuous end to the relationship between two great NBA players, and many wondered out loud just how many championships they had left on the table due to their inability to work together any longer.

They continued to feud, though it was mostly O'Neal who made comments about wanting to have more championships than

Bryant. By the end of both of their professional careers, Bryant had collected two more championship rings, and O'Neal was only able to gather one more, giving Bryant the edge, 5-4.

O'Neal, to his credit, had three NBA Finals MVPs to Bryant's two, and they both had one league MVP each. Both players were selected to the Basketball Hall of Fame, as well. Kobe Bryant passed away in 2020 in a helicopter accident, leaving O'Neal wishing they had mended their relationship sooner.

Two champions were lucky enough to be teammates for several years in the prime of their careers. However, their egos and attitudes could not be overcome. They were able to win three championships in the best basketball league in the world, but they were arguably capable of so much more.

Their legacy is a mixed one, but the basketball world was still fortunate to see their greatness. Even if it was too short of a time, their impact on the game lasts to this day.

# Larry's Incredible Putback

Larry Bird is considered one of the NBA's greatest players of all time. He was well known in his time for the incredible skill he often displayed, which went well with the trash-talking he liked to utilize as he beat his opponents.

On this particular evening during the 1981 NBA Finals, Bird demonstrated his supreme understanding of the game in a strange but miraculous way. Let's take a look at the situation in Game 1. There were a few minutes left on the clock, and Larry Bird's Boston Celtics were trailing the Houston Rockets by three points. There was still time, but mistakes could be costly.

As the Celtics came down the court with the ball, Larry Bird was about to make one of those potentially costly mistakes. He put up a jump shot from 18 feet out, and every other player on the court turned toward the basket to contest a possible rebound.

However, Larry Bird was not watching the rim. He was calculating. He knew from the moment the ball had left his fingers, maybe even sooner, that it was not going in. He also knew where the ball was headed once it struck the rim.

Bird sprinted toward the baseline behind the backboard, and sure enough, the ball deflected off the rim and bounced toward the baseline, right where Bird was heading. He was able to corral the ball with his right hand, but he didn't have a clean shot, as he was behind the backboard. Instead, he shifted the ball to his left hand, reached backward with it, and pushed the ball up toward the rim once more.

Amazingly, in that single smooth motion behind the backboard, Larry Bird had guided the ball up and into the net. Many of the fans in the arena were stunned by what they had seen. They had barely processed his missed jumper!

After, the Celtics' General Manager, Red Auerbach, declared that Bird's shot was "one of the best shots I've ever seen a player make."

The Celtics would go on to win Game 1 of the series, and although the series went six games, Bird and his teammates emerged victorious. It was the beginning of a decade featuring Bird and the Celtics as they battled the Los Angeles Lakers for NBA supremacy.

For many, the remarkable shot by Larry Bird was a sign that he was going to be a star in the league for a very long time, and indeed he was. By the end of his Hall of Fame career, Bird had three championship rings, two NBA Finals MVP honors, along with three league MVP awards.

He would go on to coach in the league as well, and as of 2024, he still works as a consultant with the Indiana Pacers. His career was just as great as that shot, although not always as fancy.

# The Dream Team

Although basketball had been an Olympic event since the 1930s, the United States team did not always dominate the competition. In fact, during the 1988 Olympics, the Americans were defeated in the semifinals, having to settle for the bronze medal. Part of this was because the American team only used amateur players, while other teams used the best players from their professional leagues.

Then, a rule change from international basketball's board of delegates in 1989 allowed the use of professional players from the NBA in international tournaments, including the Olympics. From there, American basketball fans began to speculate which NBA players would make the team.

Although many of the selections were expected, such as Michael Jordan, Karl Malone, John Stockton, Charles Barkley, and Patrick Ewing, there were a few small surprises. Larry Bird was selected to the team despite a lingering back issue that had been hampering the later years of his career.

Another surprise selection was Magic Johnson, who had retired from the Los Angeles Lakers just months before due to his very public HIV diagnosis.

Also, notably, one college player was selected. Christian Laettner was picked over Shaquille O'Neal, partly because his coach at Duke University, Coach K, was also a member of the coaching staff for Team USA.

With the roster set, the team traveled to the Olympics, where they were promptly treated like basketball royalty. Players from around the world approached Team USA players for autographs and pictures.

The team didn't even stay at the Olympic Village with the rest of the competitors, opting instead for a private hotel because of all the attention they were attracting.

With all of the hype, the only thing left for the team to do was play the Games. And, as expected, it was a slaughter. In fact, the most interesting game that took place was in the lead-up to the tournament, as Team USA divided into two groups for a scrimmage.

Michael Jordan would call that game the best game he had ever played in.

As for the tournament games, well, Team USA opened the tournament with a 68-point victory over Angola. Then, they defeated Croatia by 33, Germany by 43, Brazil by 44, and Spain by 41 to win Group A and advance to the quarterfinals.

From there, it was more destruction. They beat Puerto Rico by 38 in the quarterfinals, then they defeated Lithuania in the semifinals by 51. In the gold medal game, they faced Croatia once again, defeating them by 32.

Charles Barkley led the team in scoring, averaging 18 points per game. It was a rout of a tournament, and it re-established the United States as the best country in the world at basketball.

The results also helped more people understand the HIV and AIDS epidemic, as Magic Johnson's inclusion showed that people with the disease were not to be feared and shunned.

It was an important tournament result, increasing the popularity of the sport around the world and helping it grow into the international phenomenon it is today.

# A Basketball Quiz

1. Only three NBA players have received Defensive Player of the Year awards four times. Which of these is not one of them?

   A. Dikembe Mutombo
   B. Ben Wallace
   C. Rudy Gobert
   D. Dwight Howard

2. The Los Angeles Lakers hold the NBA record for consecutive wins with how many?

   A. 29
   B. 33
   C. C. 35D. 38

3. Only one player has won the Scoring Title and Defensive Player of the Year in the same season. Who was it?

   A. Karl Malone
   B. Michael Jordan
   C. Patrick Ewing
   D. Charles Barkley

4. The oldest MVP winner was Karl Malone, during the 1999 season. How old was he when he won it?

   A. 35
   B. 36
   C. C. 37D. 38

5. Which player was the only one to play across four different decades, for a total of 22 seasons?

   A. LeBron James

B.  Dirk Nowitzki

C.  Vince Carter

D.  Yao Ming

6.  **Wilt Chamberlain and Michael Jordan are tied for the most consecutive seasons leading the league in total points scored. For how many seasons did they do it?**

A.  Five

B.  Six

C.  Seven

D.  Eight

7.  **Which NBA legend has missed more field goal attempts than any other player in league history?**

A.  Michael Jordan

B.  Russell Westbrook

C.  James Harden

D.  Kobe Bryant

8.  **Shaquille O'Neal led the NBA in shooting percentage for how many years, more than any other player?**

A.  Seven

B.  Eight

C.  Nine

D.  Ten

9.  **Which prolific passer has more career assists than any other player, and it's not particularly close?**

A.  John Stockton

B.  Jason Kidd

C.  Chris Paul

D.  LeBron James

10. **Which dominant center leads the NBA in career blocks?**

A. Kareem Abdul-Jabbar
B. Hakeem Olajuwon
C. Dikembe Mutombo
D. Mark Eaton

# CHAPTER 6
# EUROPEAN FOOTBALL

# A Brief History of European Football

While there have been ball-kicking games around for thousands of years, the formation of European football, or association football, occurred in the middle of the 19th century thanks initially to rulesets like the Cambridge rules. With several rule sets popping up around the English-speaking world, the formation of The Football Association in 1863 sought to develop a comprehensive set of rules for the game.

The "Laws of the Game" were issued in December 1863, forbidding running with the ball in one's hands and kicking another player in the shins. Many of these rules caused some of the clubs to split away from the sport and form rugby unions instead.

Nine years later, the FA Cup took place for the first time in 1872, making it the oldest European football competition. That same year also marked the first international contest between England and Scotland.

In 1886, the International Football Association Board was established, helping to maintain and determine the Laws of the Game. The International Federation of Association Football (FIFA) was formed in 1904, which also helped to spread the game around the world. By 1930, the World Cup became an established international tournament of nations.

Today, the sport is the most popular in the world. It is easily the most accessible; if you've got a ball, 22 people can participate at once. International contests and popular European and South American leagues dominate the scene, creating superstars at every turn.

The women's game has also come a long way in the last 40 years. The Women's World Cup was first held in 1991, and women's leagues have begun growing in Europe, North America, and South America.

# Fun European Football Facts

1. The first use of yellow and red cards occurred during the 1970 FIFA World Cup.
2. As of 2024, there are 211 teams eligible to compete for World Cup qualification.
3. Official balls have a circumference between 27 and 28 inches.
4. The Champions League was founded in 1955, and it crowns a European champion every year.
5. El Salvador and Honduras fought each other in the Football War. Though they faced each other in a 1970 World Cup qualifier that also involved rioting, the true cause of the war was not the sporting event.
6. Only eight countries have ever won the World Cup, and Brazil has won the most of any country, with five.
7. Only seven teams have ever won the Premier League, which was founded in 1992.
8. Lionel Messi's 474 goals are the most of any scorer in the history of La Liga.
9. Cristiano Ronaldo holds several Champions League records, including appearances, goals, and assists.
10. Bayern Munich has won the Bundesliga 33 times, which is 24 more than the next closest team on the list, FC Nurnberg.

# Great European Football Stories

## Zidane Volleys a Championship

European football has a lot of different tournaments. None are bigger than the Champions League, which brings together the top teams from all of the European leagues. When this tournament takes place, fans watch and hope that their star players can rise to the occasion.

The 2002 Champions League Final holds one of these great examples.

You see, Zinedine Zidane was a member of Real Madrid, one of the two teams involved in the 2002 Champions League Final, and he was considered a great player. He had won the World Cup with France in 1998, even scoring twice in the Final. A few years later, he joined Real Madrid to help them reach the pinnacle of European football, the Champions League.

And in 2002, the team had that chance.

While Zidane was trending toward the end of his dominance, as he was over 30 years old, he still had a bit of magic to share with his team.

With the score tied at one goal each, and the clock ticking down toward the end of the first half, Zinedine Zidane had an opportunity to strike, and it came from quite the unlikely scenario. Santiago Solari of Madrid sent the ball down the sideline toward Roberto Carlos, who challenged for the ball against Zoltan Sebescen of Bayer Leverkusen, their opponents in the Final. Carlos reached the ball first, but his first touch on the ball was a surprising one. Instead of trying to control it or direct it to himself, he instead flicked the ball high into the air toward the top of the box.

The ball floated in the air for four seconds - a very long time in the sport of football - but there was only one player under it who was ready to strike.

Zinedine Zidane was the only player there, leaving him enough space to volley the ball as it returned to the ground. It was a blistering shot that curved very little as it found the upper corner at the near post, sending the spectators into a frenzy of cheers and applause. Real Madrid had the lead going into halftime thanks to Zidane.

Real Madrid would hold on to that lead and win the 2002 Champions League Final, adding the trophy to their collection and further bolstering Zidane's legacy as one of the best French players of all time.

Another more infamous moment tarnished some of that legacy for Zidane, but that is a story for you to explore on your own.

# The 2005 Champions League Final

European football matches are played in two halves. Sometimes, a football match can also be a tale of two halves, meaning that each tells a very different story. It is amazing how one team who does so well in the first half of a match, can sometimes collapse or run out of gas in the second half. It is equally amazing to see a team fall behind big in the first half only to recover and win.

This is the story of the 2005 Champions League final between Liverpool and Milan.

In the first half of the match, Milan played just like the contenders they had proven themselves to be during the rest of the tournament. It only took one minute for Milan to strike, and they did so thanks to a free kick from Andrea Pirlo, which connected with team captain Paolo Maldini in the middle of the box for a volley to the far post.

Then, late in the first half, Kaka made a great pass to Andriy Shevchenko, who had an opportunity to shoot but passed it to Hernan Crespo. Crespo finished off the play and easily slotted the ball into the goal, doubling Milan's lead.

If Liverpool thought it couldn't get worse, they were wrong. Just five minutes later, in the 44th minute, Kaka and Crespo combined again, this time ending with a Crespo chip over Jerzy Dudek and into the goal.

It was a three-goal lead in the Champions League Final.

A Steven Gerrard header put Liverpool on the board in the 54th minute, which was a good start, but there was so much more work to do. Milan likely wasn't ready to panic, but two minutes after Gerrard's goal, Vladimir Smicer scored a long-range goal to cut the lead down to one.

Just three minutes later, Liverpool was awarded a penalty when Gerrard was fouled in the box. Xabi Alonso's first shot was stopped, but he was able to slot home the rebound. By the 61st minute, the match was tied. In a matter of 15 minutes, Liverpool had completely turned the tide of the match.

The match remained tied after that mayhem to start the second half. The two teams battled through extra time to reach penalty kicks. Needing only four shooters, Liverpool won the penalty kicks 3-2, taking the Champions League crown and completing one of the most incredible comebacks in football history.

# Watford's Final Chance

It is always exciting when a team scores a goal in the final moments of a match. It is even better when the match is one of great consequence. Leicester City had this moment during a match against Watford back in 2013. The two teams were competing in the 2013 Football League Championship Playoff semifinal. The winner of the two-leg matchup would advance to the Playoff final, and the winner of the playoff would be promoted to the Premier League, the top league in England.

In the first leg, Leicester City won 1-0 at home, sending the match to Watford for the second leg. If Leicester City could draw, they would advance in the tournament and be one step closer to promotion.

As the match came closer to its conclusion, Watford was winning the leg 2-1, but because they conceded an away goal, Watford was losing the tiebreaker. Leicester could lose the second leg 2-1 and still advance, so they were in the driver's seat.

Their situation improved even further when Anthony Knockaert earned a penalty kick in stoppage time. It was a golden opportunity to go up 3-1 and put Watford away for good. The Watford crowd did not like the call, as it looked as if Knockaert had gone to ground a bit too easily.

Regardless, all Watford's fans could do was sit and watch in despair as Knockaert lined up to take his shot.

Then, a save! Watford fans did not even have a chance to cheer, though, as the rebound came right back to Knockaert, who followed up to take another shot. Another save! The home crowd exploded in cheers, even though they knew a victory was still unlikely. Their season would last a few more seconds.

But the ball was moving up the field. Watford had numbers forward for the attack. The crowd buzzed in anticipation as they hoped against hope for a miracle on the field.

Fernando Forestieri ran the ball down the sideline and created space for himself to get a cross into the box, and at the far post, Jonathan Hogg was able to get his head on it. The Watford crowd rose to their feet as Hogg jumped up, but he didn't head the ball towards the goal. Instead, he directed the ball back to the middle of the box, where a sprinting Troy Deeney was ready to fire.

Deeney struck the ball hard and true, rocketing it into the goal and causing mayhem on the field. The fans rushed the field and celebrated with their team, as Watford was on their way to the playoff final.

It was an incredible moment for Watford, to snatch victory from the jaws of defeat in the final moments of the playoff match.

Watford would go on to lose in the final of that playoff, but both teams would eventually earn promotion to the Premier League, and Leicester would win the league soon after.

It may not have been the storybook ending to the tournament, but the magical moment that took place in those final seconds created great memories for the fans in the stadium that day.

# The 1994 World Cup Final

Roberto Baggio was one of the world's best football players during the 1980s and 90s. He joined Juventus in 1990, scoring 78 goals over 141 appearances with the squad over his career. With his success on the professional stage, he began garnering interest from his national team, Italy.

During the 1990 World Cup, Baggio scored twice for Italy as the team reached the semi-finals before losing to Argentina. It was a strong performance for the young player, and Italy's fans were excited to see him progress and return in 1994.

Sure enough, Baggio was on the roster for Italy, and he had only improved during that four-year gap. He was the captain of Juventus, and he even scored twice to help his squad win the UEFA Cup Final over Borussia Dortmund.

In the buildup to the 1994 tournament, Baggio scored five goals for the team, helping to make qualification a certainty. With all of this strong play, though, expectations began to grow. All of Italy was ready for their team to win the World Cup, and many fans saw Roberto Baggio as the key to victory.

Unfortunately for Baggio and the team, there were early signs that the pressure and expectation might be a little too much for them to handle. To open group play in the tournament, Italy lost to the Republic of Ireland in a surprising 1-0 defeat. The Italian team had several chances to score during that match, but their chances to advance in the tournament were significantly reduced.

A 1-0 victory over Norway helped to get the ship turned around, but a draw against Mexico to finish the group stage left them third in the group. However, because they had one of the better records among third-place teams, they made it to the knockout stage. Of course, anything could happen from there.

Roberto Baggio was determined to keep his team in this tournament, though. In the first knockout stage, Italy faced Nigeria, and they fell behind in the 25th minute. The game continued late into the second half before Baggio scored the equalizer in the 88th minute, sending the match into extra time. There, Baggio scored a penalty kick in the 102nd minute, helping to seal the victory for Italy.

He would score in the 88th minute of the quarterfinals to give Italy a 2-1 victory over Spain, too. In case you thought this was good enough, he scored both of Italy's goals, in a span of four minutes, to defeat Bulgaria 2-1 in the semifinals.

Leading up to the 1994 World Cup Final, Roberto Baggio had almost singlehandedly carried Italy through the knockout stages to reach the pinnacle of the tournament. Then, against Brazil, the match remained scoreless through extra time, requiring a shootout.

It was then that Italy's luck ran out. Roberto Baggio couldn't carry the team through a shootout. Baggio was Italy's fifth shooter, and he needed to make his shot to keep his team alive. However, his penalty went over the crossbar.

Brazil won the World Cup, and Roberto Baggio was left wondering how much more he could have done. Regardless, it was an incredible run that ended in heartbreak.

## Aguero's Last-Minute Goal

When it comes to football league championships, the winners can often be decided several days, or even weeks, before the conclusion of the season. One team can run away with their lead in the standings and make it mathematically impossible for anyone to catch them, regardless of the results on the pitch.

Then there are days like the May 13, 2012, the final day of the 2011–2012 Premier League season. Going into the final day of that season, two teams were tied atop the league standings. Manchester United and Manchester City were deadlocked at 86 points each. They had identical records, but Manchester City had a substantial lead in the tiebreaker, the goal differential.

If Manchester City won, they would clinch the title regardless of Manchester United's result. If United won and City did anything but win, then United would win the league.

Both teams were playing at the same time, but they were not playing each other. Manchester United was playing against Sunderland, a mid-table team with little to play for at the end of the season. Manchester City, however, was playing Queens Park Rangers, a team desperate for a victory to escape relegation.

Fans all over the country watched the dueling games to see how the exciting moment would play out.

Wayne Rooney scored a goal for United 20 minutes into their match, taking a 1-0 lead. City scored against QPR in the 39th minute thanks to Pablo Zabaleta, and both matches went to halftime with those 1-0 scores. If those scores held, then City would win the league.

Then, disaster struck for City. Djibril Cisse scored for QPR in the 48th minute, leveling the match. A red card for QPR gave City hope again, but 11 minutes later, Jamie Mackie scored again, giving QPR a shocking lead with 24 minutes remaining.

The Manchester United match with Sunderland had an uneventful second half, ending in that 1-0 score. City needed a miracle as the minutes ticked away. Then, into stoppage time, the miracle, or miracles, came.

Edin Dzeko, who had come on in the 69th minute for Gareth Barry, connected with a powerful header that found its way into the goal, but it was already the second minute of stoppage time. The match was tied, but City needed one more.

In the 94th minute, Sergio Aguero collected a pass about 35 yards away from goal, then passed off to Mario Balotelli. Balotelli went down from a challenging defender, but while lying on his back, he poked at the ball to dispossess his opponent, giving the ball back to Aguero, who used the surprised defenders to his advantage. He avoided three attackers before firing a ball at the goal.

Goalkeeper Paddy Kenny couldn't get a hand on it as the ball sneaked inside the near post and into the goal, sending Manchester City and its stadium into a frenzy. Meanwhile, Manchester United could be seen saluting their fans, even as they heard the news that they would not be league champions that season.

It was an incredible moment for the Premier League, one that is still widely celebrated to this day. It was City's first championship since 1968, and it served as a strong signal that a new team belonged among the ranks of the best teams in the country.

# The 1988 FA Cup Final

The FA Cup is a tournament that features over 700 teams, each of which competes in domestic English football. It is a 12-round tournament that is drawn randomly, meaning that some of the biggest teams in the country can play against some of the smallest squads from the lowest tiers of English football.

Of course, when this tournament happens, it is most often the biggest, best teams that rise to the top. The Final of the tournament is almost always a contest between two teams from the top tier of the professional leagues, but every once in a great while, a team from the lower ranks can score a surprising win. It gives that small team bragging rights, and fans of that team will tell the story for years and decades to come.

One such magnificent story took place during the 1988 FA Cup. Wimbledon had quickly been promoted up the leagues over the past nine years, even finishing the top league in seventh place. Continuing their strong play and wondering when the moves up the ladder might stop, Wimbledon used their aggressive style to their advantage and reached the 1988 FA Cup Final!

On the other side of the bracket, though, was a traditional powerhouse of English football, Liverpool. They were coming off a league championship, and their style of play was much more elegant - and much more in line with how English football fans liked the game played.

It was quite the shock, then, when Wimbledon opened the scoring in the 37th minute thanks to a header from Lawrie Sanchez. From then on, Liverpool increased their offensive pressure and searched desperately for an equalizing goal.

In the 60<sup>th</sup> minute, Liverpool had their golden opportunity when John Aldridge was fouled in the penalty area by Clive Goodyear. However, the ensuing penalty kick was saved by Wimbledon keeper Dave Beasant, a stunning moment that almost seemed to doom Liverpool to their fate. As the final moments ticked away, Wimbledon withstood the pressure and held on for the 1-0 victory, stunning all of England with the win.

It was a moment in English football history that will live on for years to come, and it showed that the beautiful game of football doesn't always have to be beautiful to get a great result on the pitch.

These days, Liverpool remains one of the top clubs in the Premier League, and Wimbledon F.C. actually dissolved in 2004, though there is another team in that city by the name of AFC Wimbledon, who finished tenth in EFL League Two in 2023–24.

Wimbledon's time at the top of English football was not long, but it was still a sweet moment that many of their fans will cherish forever.

# A European Football Quiz

1. Who holds the record for scoring the most goals over the course of a single calendar year? A hint: the record was set in 2012.

    A. Cristiano Ronaldo
    B. Lionel Messi
    C. Juninho
    D. Robert Lewandowski

2. From 1966 to 1997, English player Peter Shilton played in how many games, more than any other player?

    A. 951
    B. 1,169
    C. 1,390
    D. 1,446

3. Only one player has won 16 international club titles. Who was it?

    A. Toni Kroos
    B. Roberto Carlos
    C. Cristiano Ronaldo
    D. Gareth Bale

4. Which Spanish national player has won more international games than any other player in FIFA history?

    A. Fernando Torres
    B. David Villa
    C. Andres Iniesta
    D. Sergio Ramos

5. What is the oldest active club in the history of the sport, dating back to 1848?

   A. Manchester United
   B. Celtic
   C. Sheffield
   D. Real Madrid

6. The longest penalty shootout in football history took place in 2024 between Dimona and Shimshon Tel Aviv. How many penalties did it take to find a winner?

   A. 26
   B. 35
   C. 49
   D. 56

7. Belfast Celtic holds the record for most consecutive wins across all competitions, set in 1947–48. How many games did they win?

   A. 31
   B. 32
   C. 33
   D. 34

8. Bayern Munich holds the record for scoring at least one goal in how many straight matches?

   A. 61
   B. 63
   C. C. 73D. 85

9. As of 2023, which player's transfer garnered the most money? Hint: He was transferred from Barcelona to Paris Saint-Germain in 2017.

   A. Neymar

B.  Kylian Mbappe

C.  Philippe Coutinho

D.  Antoine Griezmann

10. **During the 2002 World Cup, Hakan Suker scored a goal in 11 seconds for which team, the fastest goal in World Cup history?**

A.  South Korea

B.  Turkey (Türkiye)

C.  Romania

D.  Japan

# CHAPTER 7
# AMERICAN FOOTBALL

# A Short History of American Football

American football's history began closely entangled with rugby in the mid-1800s. However, the game began to take its own shape thanks to American Walter Camp, who contributed to the game enough to be known as the "Father of American Football."

For example, Camp developed the downs system, limiting how many chances an offense would have to advance the ball a certain number of yards. While the modern game gives four downs to get ten yards, the initial rule gave three downs to get five yards.

The early years of the sport were difficult in many respects, but one of the biggest ones was the violence. In 1905, 19 players died around the country from playing football, leading to threats from American President Theodore Roosevelt to abolish the game unless more rule changes were implemented.

One year later, the forward pass was introduced to the sport.

A group of professional teams first came together in 1920, known now as the NFL, and it did not take long for the league to establish itself as the top organization for professional play in the country.

While the NFL was growing quickly, many still viewed college football as the dominant form of the game. This was the case until the 1930s, when increased passing in the NFL helped distinguish it from the college game, helping the NFL grow even more.

In 1960, the American Football League was introduced to challenge the NFL for professional football dominance, using money to buy some of the better players and recruit them before NFL teams could.

Ten years later, the two leagues merged, which is why the current NFL is separated into two conferences. Since then, teams have been added to expand the league into its current form.

As for college football, where the game first started, it has never been more popular in the United States. Universities from all over the country compete for the chance to be a national champion, and millions of fans watch along. As of 2023, only four teams from the 100+ top division schools can qualify for the playoff, and even many of those teams are ranked partially on reputation, which takes accomplishments away from smaller schools that may outperform expectations from year to year.

Football has come quite a long way since its inception, and it has done nothing but grow in popularity. Though there is still controversy regarding the physical and mental effects on the players, the game continues to improve and change to make it safe.

Most recently, American football changed the rules for kickoffs to prevent players from opposing teams sprinting across the field to hit each other during those plays. It may make the game a little less exciting, as breaking a run for a kickoff touchdown is less likely now, but it is a good step to take care of the players and their fans.

American football has remained an imperfect sport throughout its history, but the leagues and organizations in charge are doing what they can to keep moving it forward.

# Fun American Football Facts

1. Four NFL teams, as of 2024, have not reached the Super Bowl. Those teams are Detroit, Cleveland, Jacksonville, and Houston.
2. Helmets were not required protection for the NFL until 1943, 23 years after the league had formed.
3. Of the 30 most-watched television shows in the United States, 27 of those shows have been NFL Super Bowls, with Super Bowl LVIII at the top of the list, as of February 2024.
4. Mark Moseley is the only NFL kicker to win the league MVP award, which he accomplished in a strike-shortened season back in 1982.
5. Ed Sabol is the oldest person to be inducted into the Hall of Fame, at 94 years old.
6. The Chicago Bears have retired 13 numbers from play, more than any other team in history. Four teams have never retired a number, and the Saints un-retired the only two numbers they had previously retired.
7. Adrian Peterson's 296 rushing yards in one game, the NFL record, was set in only his eighth game in the league.
8. Jerry Rice and Brett Favre are the only two non-kickers to play in more than 300 NFL games.
9. The NFL record for fewest interceptions by a team during one season was four, set by the New England Patriots in 2010.
10. Hall of Fame inductee Eli Manning had a career win-loss record of 118 and 118.

# Great American Football Stories

## Boise State's Tricky Win

The 2006 Boise State University Broncos football team knew they had a chance to do something special. They had more returning starters than any other college team in the country, and they had been winning consistently for a few years.

It was no surprise to them, then, when they finished the 2006 season undefeated. While they were not awarded a spot in the National Championship game because of a perceived weaker schedule, they were granted an opportunity to face off against the Oklahoma Sooners, a team ranked seventh at the time, in the Fiesta Bowl.

Although Oklahoma did not have a perfect record, they were still considered the favorites over the smaller school of Boise State. That did not matter to the Broncos, who pulled out all the stops to remain competitive during the game. In fact, Boise State relied on their high-powered offense to build up an 11-point lead at halftime.

But Oklahoma would not go down quietly. The Sooners rallied in the second half, and they were able to tie the game at 28 before taking the lead, 35-28 thanks to an interception returned for a touchdown.

With their backs against the wall, Boise State had less than a minute to score if they wanted to send the game to overtime. They worked the ball to midfield but only had 18 seconds left. They needed a trick, so they pulled one out of the bag. In what is known as a "hook and ladder" play, they passed the ball downfield to a receiver in the middle of the field. As defenders closed on the player with the ball, he pitched it to a teammate streaking across the field laterally, giving him an extra boost to get around the defenders running the wrong way.

It worked, and Boise State scored with seven seconds left in the game, sending it to overtime.

Oklahoma started the overtime on offense, and a touchdown from running back Adrian Peterson gave them a 42-35 lead. Boise would have to score a touchdown and an extra point to extend the game.

With a passing touchdown, Boise accomplished exactly what they needed, but then the game announcers noticed some peculiar movement on the field after the touchdown.

The Boise State Broncos were not setting up for an extra point. They were going for the two-point conversion - and the win!

They came to the line of scrimmage with the quarterback under center, running back in the backfield, and a bunch formation of receivers to his right. When the ball was snapped, the quarterback took his dropback steps and faked a throw toward the cluster of receivers.

Instead of letting go of the ball, he followed through the throwing motion and then held the ball behind his back, allowing his running back to take it and run to the end zone on the opposite side of the receivers.

It was executed to perfection, and the 2006 Boise State Broncos ended their season undefeated, with a Fiesta Bowl victory under their belts. They proved to the college football world that smaller schools are capable of beating bigger schools, changing the landscape of college football forever.

# The Helmet Catch

There are only a handful of NFL games that have their own nicknames based on events in the game. The Helmet Catch game is one of the most well-known in recent memory. It was a Super Bowl matchup between two teams that had experienced very different regular seasons. The New York Giants had finished the season with a 10-6 record, barely sneaking into the playoffs and never playing a home game on their way to Super Bowl XLII.

Their opponents, the New England Patriots, had just finished the season 16-0, and they were looking to become the second team in NFL history to finish a perfect season. Because of this dominance that New England had demonstrated, they were the favorites going into the championship game.

Eli Manning of the Giants and Tom Brady of the Patriots were both looking to lead their teams to victory, but the entire game would come down to one near-impossible catch.

The entire game was much more closely contested than anyone could have imagined. The Giants had a 3-0 lead at the end of the first quarter, but the Patriots responded in the second quarter with a touchdown, taking a 7-3 lead to halftime.

The third quarter was scoreless, sending the game to the fourth quarter, where the Giants took the lead thanks to a David Tyree touchdown catch. It was 10-7 with 11 minutes left in the game, but New England would have their chance to complete the perfect season.

After each team failed on a drive, the Patriots put together an 11-play drive to score the go-ahead touchdown with less than three minutes remaining. It was not a lot of time, but there was still a chance for the Giants.

Things were looking especially shaky when Manning nearly threw an interception that fell through the hands of a New England defender. On the next play, third down and five from the Giants' 44-yard line, the incredible play took place.

Manning took the ball from shotgun and had to scramble away from rushing defenders. He escaped the pressure and threw up a prayer down the middle of the field where David Tyree was standing and waiting for the ball. As the ball arrived, so did a New England defender. Both players jumped up for the ball, but Tyree got his hands on it first.

However, he couldn't bring his hands down to secure the ball into his body because of the New England defender. Instead, he pinned the ball against the crown of his helmet as both players fell to the ground. Miraculously, he held the ball tight against his helmet, unwilling to let the defender strip it away.

The Giants were at the Patriots' 25-yard line, and three plays later, they were in the end zone. Eli Manning and the Giants went on to defeat the New England Patriots and ruin their perfect season, but nothing short of a miraculous Helmet Catch could get it done against Brady and the Patriots.

It was an incredible finish to an incredible game, and the only perfect season in football history, the 1972 Miami Dolphins, continued to celebrate their exclusive club.

# The Perfect Season

American football is a brutally difficult game. With 22 players on the field at any time, there are plenty of variables capable of turning the tide of the game toward one team or another. Because of this, winning games is a difficult task, even when one team is more skilled than the other.

Only one team in NFL history has successfully won every regular season and playoff game on their way to a Super Bowl championship, and that is the 1972 Miami Dolphins. It was a season that was carried, almost quite literally, by their two running backs, Larry Csonka and Mercury Morris. The two backs combined to score a substantial percentage of the team's points throughout the season, which was very helpful considering what happened to Bob Griese, their starting quarterback.

In Week 5, Griese suffered a broken ankle, leaving the quarterbacking duties to veteran Earl Morrall. While Morrall's performance was not great, he limited his mistakes to keep his offense on the field.

It also helped that the "No-Name Defense," so named by the Dallas Cowboys' coach, Tom Landry, was one of the most dominant units in the sport's history.

In total, the 1972 Dolphins had nine players selected to the Pro Bowl at the end of the season, and four of them were named AP All-Pros.

Still, it was not an easy path, and anything can happen in the playoffs. In fact, many analysts wondered what would happen when Griese returned from injury, which happened toward the end of the regular season.

The team decided to keep Morrall in as quarterback until the second half of the AFC Championship game. Griese helped keep the Dolphins' offense on the field longer as they withstood the comeback attempt from the Pittsburgh Steelers.

Then, in the Super Bowl game, the Dolphins had to take on the Washington Redskins to complete their perfect season. They took a 14-0 lead into halftime, frustrating the Redskins offense and completely shutting them down.

The only points that the Redskins put on the board were in the fourth quarter, when their special teams unit blocked a Dolphins field goal and returned it for a touchdown. By that time, though, it was late in the fourth quarter, leaving Miami the task of running out the clock and sealing their perfect season.

The 1972 Dolphins remain, to this day, the only NFL team to ever finish a season with complete perfection. They won all 14 regular season games, and their three playoff games. Many of the players from that team often toast the end of another NFL season with no other team able to repeat the feat.

And as the league becomes more level in terms of talent, there is a good chance that no team ever matches that record.

# The 2013 Iron Bowl

College football has developed some great rivalries over the 100+ years of its history, as universities close to each other in terms of geography tended to play each other annually. One of those great rivalries is known as the Iron Bowl, which is played between Alabama and Auburn, two colleges that were particularly strong football programs in the 2010s.

When these two teams met for the 2013 Iron Bowl, the game had implications for the National Championship, too. The winner would likely be one of the two teams in that title game if they finished out their season with wins, so the Iron Bowl was an important one.

Late in the fourth quarter, Auburn scored a touchdown with seven seconds left in the game, knotting the score at 28. On the ensuing kickoff, though, Alabama got the ball down to Auburn's 38-yard line. Although Auburn tried to run out the clock, the referees determined that the Alabama player stepped out of bounds with one second left on the clock.

Alabama decided they would kick a 57-yard field goal, which was a questionable decision when paired with who they sent out to kick it. Their regular kicker, Cade Foster, had already missed three kicks earlier in the game, so they sent out freshman Adam Griffith.

Auburn, for their part, lined up ten men near the line of scrimmage, but they left one defender in their end zone, just in case the kick came up short and could be returned.

After timeouts to ice the kicker, Griffith put everything he could into the kick. As it flew through the air, the Alabama blockers watched in hope. They did not notice the Auburn defenders repositioning in preparation for the runback.

Sure enough, the ball fell short and into the arms of Chris Davis, who ran out of the endzone with it. As he ran up the middle of the field, he decided to run to his left and angle toward the sideline. As he tiptoed up the line, his teammates came up with two massive blocks to give him the path he needed.

The crowd exploded in cheers and screams as they watched Davis run to the end zone with no one in the way to stop him. Auburn had defeated the top-ranked team in the country, putting themselves in the driver's seat to reach the National Championship.

It was one of the more magical finishes to any football game. It is rare for one team to be so close to winning the game, only for the other team to turn the tables in an instant and win the game at the last possible moment.

Auburn would go on to lose in the National Championship against Florida State, 34-31, but it was a close game between two great teams. Regardless of the ultimate outcome, Auburn stunned the football world with that magnificent finish to the 2013 Iron Bowl.

# The Immaculate Reception

Earning a spot in a Super Bowl can be a difficult task for any team. Sometimes, you need a little bit of luck to go your way. Few teams have ever been as lucky as the Pittsburgh Steelers were during the battle to reach the 1972 AFC Championship game as they faced the Oakland Raiders.

They were so lucky, in fact, that the play in question is called the "Immaculate Reception," a play on words referencing the Immaculate Conception, the miracle of Jesus' birth in the Christian Bible.

This miracle took place in the second half of a scoreless contest, in which both teams were struggling offensively while their defenses were stealing the show. The Steelers finally broke the tie with a field goal in the third quarter, which they followed up with one more field goal as the game entered the fourth quarter.

When Raiders coach John Madden made a change at quarterback, it helped the Raiders offense find some life, and that translated to a 30-yard quarterback scramble for the go-ahead touchdown with just over a minute left in the game. Leading 7-6, the Raiders defense just needed one more stop.

It seemed like the Raiders would get that stop, too. With 22 seconds left in the game, the Steelers were facing a fourth-and-ten from their own side of midfield. Against those odds, considering the defensive battle both teams had been in all game, it was nearly safe to say that the game was over.

The Steelers ran a play to target their rookie wide receiver, Barry Pearson, in the hopes of catching the Raiders off guard. However, once the ball was snapped, quarterback Terry

Bradshaw had to scramble away and throw the ball as far as he could down the field.

The ball was headed toward halfback John Fuqua, but before it got to him, it hit the helmet of Raiders safety Jack Tatum. The ball ricocheted into the air, where Steelers fullback Franco Harris ran up and barely caught the ball, inches from the ground.

Using his momentum and the confusion of several players on the field, Harris blew by one defender, then got a helpful block from one of his teammates as he scampered 40 yards and into the endzone.

Then, a bit of controversy. One referee signaled a touchdown, but other referees were not convinced by what they had seen. Was it an illegal lateral, or had the ball touched the ground before the catch?

The head referee called the NFL's officials supervisor and told him the situation. They agreed it should be ruled a touchdown.

The Pittsburgh Steelers went on to win the game 13-7. Their luck ran out in the AFC Championship when they lost to the undefeated Miami Dolphins.

While the call remains controversial to some, others appreciate the incredible luck on the play. Some believe the referee used video replay to look at the play. If so, it would have been the first play in NFL history to use this technology. However, the referee denied that this ever happened and there is no confirmation that video replay was used.

Still, it was an amazing play with plenty of football history packed into it.

## One Yard Short

The Super Bowl is the pinnacle of American pop culture almost every year. It is a big moment for football teams and their fans, and that big game often comes down to mere inches.

One such Super Bowl had that epic finish, and it took place in January of 1999. The two teams facing off were the Tennessee Titans and the St. Louis Rams, and both squads were looking to capture their first Super Bowl title. The Rams were the favorites thanks to their superpowered offense, and they also had the benefit of surprising the entire league with their play, as they were not expected to do so well.

Tennessee reached the playoffs through a Wild Card spot, adding one more game to their playoff schedule. And yet, they still reached the championship thanks to quarterback Steve McNair and running back Eddie George, both of whom were capable of gaining big chunks of yards on the ground.

The first half of the contest was very one-sided, though. In yards gained, the Rams held a wide edge of 294 yards to Tennessee's 89. However, despite all of that offensive success, the Titans had successfully kept the Rams out of the endzone, only allowing three field goals.

It was a 9-0 lead for the Rams as the teams prepared for the second half.

The Titans had a field goal blocked to end their first drive of the half, and things didn't get better when the Rams finally found the endzone, taking a huge 16-0 lead. Eddie George helped the Titans get on the board finally, but they failed on the two-point conversion, leaving the score 16-6.

Into the fourth, the Titans got a defensive stop before driving 79 yards and pounding in another touchdown from George. With the score 16-13, the game was suddenly competitive.

Somehow, the Titans seemed to have figured out the Rams' offense, because they got another stop and added a field goal, tying the game with less than three minutes left in the game.

Then, a seemingly fatal error. Isaac Bruce caught a pass from Kurt Warner and took it the distance, a 73-yard touchdown to restore the Rams' lead.

The Titans got the ball back on their own 12-yard line, and less than two minutes on the clock.

It was a tall order, but McNair went to work, completing two passes before a facemask penalty gave them another 15 yards.

The Titans worked the ball down to the Rams' ten-yard line, but they were down to six seconds on the clock. With no timeouts left, they had one final chance to score the points and tie or win the game.

From shotgun, they threw to Kevin Dyson over the middle, who caught the ball at the five-yard line. However, Mike Jones had stopped covering another receiver, anticipating the play, and closing the gap on Dyson as the receiver tried to break for the goal line. Jones wrapped his arms around Dyson's lower body, trying to drag him to the ground.

Dyson began to stumble but reached the ball out for the goal line. As Dyson's knees went to the ground, the ball was one yard short of a touchdown, and the game came to a painful end, with the Rams defense playing heroes.

The final play became famous for the drama of the moment, one of the closest finishes in Super Bowl history.

# An American Football Quiz

1. Jason Hanson holds the NFL record for most seasons played with a single team. Which team?

   A. Green Bay Packers
   B. Chicago Bears
   C. Detroit Lions
   D. New England Patriots

2. Which University of Michigan running back holds the NCAA record for most consecutive rushing attempts without losing a fumble?

   A. Blake Corum
   B. Donovan Edwards
   C. Tyrone Wheatley
   D. Mike Hart

3. Keenan Reynolds, a quarterback from which university, holds the record for most rushing touchdowns in an FBS career?

   A. Army
   B. Navy
   C. Air Force
   D. Princeton

4. Which NFL great holds the record for most total touchdowns over a career, with 208?

   A. Jerry Rice
   B. Emmitt Smith
   C. LaDainian Tomlinson
   D. Randy Moss

5. As of 2021, Justin Tucker of which team holds the NFL record for the longest field goal?

   A. Washington Commanders
   B. Indianapolis Colts
   C. Denver Broncos
   D. Baltimore Ravens

6. Frank Gore holds the NFL record for most consecutive seasons rushing 500 or more yards. How many seasons did he do it?

   A. 14
   B. 15
   C. 16
   D. 17

7. Eric Dickerson holds the single season rushing yards record, but who holds the record for most rushing yards in a season without a fumble?

   A. Walter Payton
   B. Adrian Peterson
   C. Emmitt Smith
   D. Barry Sanders

8. Connor Halliday of Washington State and which Texas Tech quarterback are tied for most passing yards in a single FBS game?

   A. Graham Harrell
   B. Kliff Kingsbury
   C. Patrick Mahomes
   D. Cody Hodges

9. No FBS quarterback has thrown more touchdown passes over their college career than which Houston player?

A. Case Keenum

B. Andre Ware

C. Kevin Kolb

D. Greg Ward

10. **Drew Brees of the New Orleans Saints holds the NFL record for most consecutive games with at least one passing touchdown. How many games is his record?**

A. 48

B. 54

C. 57

D. 61

# CHAPTER 8
# BASEBALL

# A Short History of Baseball

Baseball originated from stick and ball games that came across the ocean from England.

While at first it was close to the game of rounders from the 1700s, the game of baseball began to take its own form during the 1830s and 1840s as amateur clubs were established along the east coast of the country.

While many consider baseball to be an American sport, the first official baseball game with a documented scorecard took place in Canada, in 1838.

While teams and clubs continued to develop, the first association of those clubs and teams was the National Association of Base Ball Players, which formed in 1858.

The first professional league was formed in 1871, but the National League was formed just five years later. The American League did not form until 1901, and the first World Series between the two leagues took place in 1903.

The scoring in baseball games used to be quite low, but partially thanks to rule changes that limited what pitchers could do to the baseball, scoring suddenly exploded in the 1920s. A big part of that scoring increase was credited to the arrival of power hitters like Babe Ruth onto the scene.

The first Black player to play in Major League Baseball was Jackie Robinson, though there were several negro leagues that existed throughout the 20th century.

Around the world, the sport spread quickly during both the 19th and 20th centuries, and there are many international competitions that are held today.

The game was included in the Olympics for a brief period of time, but there are also the World Baseball Classic and the Baseball World Cup for international teams to compete against one another.

Baseball was the most popular sport in the United States for the entire first half of the 20th century, but that title was lost to American football in the latter decades of the century. It is still widely played and celebrated, and Major League Baseball players are some of the highest-compensated athletes in North American sports.

# Fun Baseball Facts

1. Every baseball used in Major League Baseball is covered in a mud called Lena Blackburne Baseball Rubbing mud.
2. The average baseball in Major League Baseball only lasts between six and seven pitches.
3. Japan and South Korea both consider baseball to be the most popular sport in their countries.
4. Historian Ken Burns released a baseball documentary film in 1994 to great critical response.
5. The All-American Girls Professional Baseball League debuted in 1943, as many men were fighting in World War II.
6. Fenway Park is the oldest MLB stadium in use today, as it opened in 1912.
7. The first time players were assigned jersey numbers was in 1907.
8. The writers of "Take Me Out to the Ball Game" had never attended a baseball game before.
9. Each MLB team plays a total of 162 games every regular season, almost double the games of other professional sports like basketball and ice hockey.
10. The New York Yankees have 27 former players in the Hall of Fame, more than any other team.

# Great Baseball Stories

## The Miracle Mets

If you have ever been a fan of a bad team, you will know how painful it can be to wait as they rebuild the roster and slowly rise to compete once again. Some teams never figure it out.

Every once in a while, though, a team will go through an unexpected transformation and greatly outperform the expectations put on them by pundits and analysts. One such team was the 1969 New York Mets.

At this time, it was only the Mets' eighth year in Major League Baseball, and it was also the first year that the American and National Leagues were split into divisions. In every other year, the Mets had competed, they never finished higher than ninth out of the ten teams in the National League.

They had also never had a winning record.

As usual, they had a dismal start to the season. They were 3-7 through the first ten games, and things were not looking any better after 23 games, as they were 9-14. After the first rough patch, though, the team began finding ways to win, though they were certainly not crushing their opponents along the way.

They won nine of their next 13 games, though they were still below .500 on the season, at 21-23.

Then, from May 28 to June 10, the Mets won 11 games in a row, sweeping three different teams. As the team continued to improve, it became clear that pitcher Tom Seaver was having an amazing season, as he already had nine wins on the year.

By the end of the season, he would lead the league with 25 wins, nine of which were complete games.

Halfway through August, the Mets still found themselves trailing the Cubs by nine games. They struggled on the road, going 9-9 that month, but they were 12-1 at home, helping to close the gap with Chicago.

What helped even more was an incredible September, which saw the Mets go 23-7 and finish with the second-best record in the entire league. They made the playoffs, becoming the first expansion team in league history to accomplish the feat. Even more important to the team's existence was their attendance. They led the league with over 26,000 spectators per home game during the season.

Since it was the first year of divisions in the league, it also meant that teams had to play in a playoff to reach the World Series. They faced the Atlanta Braves, and the Mets did not expend any extra energy in that series. The Mets continued their fantastic run, sweeping the Braves to reach the World Series.

There, against the Baltimore Orioles, the Mets perhaps suffered from some early nerves, losing Game 1 by a score of 4-1. From there, though, the Mets rattled off four straight wins to win the World Series, an incredible result when their previous seasons were considered.

They put it together at the right time and made it work.

# Jackie Robinson

The culture in which a sport exists can often exert its influence on the game, controlling aspects of the sport by the power of peer pressure and the threat of losing business. Sometimes, though, a sport can act as a conduit to change the culture around it.

Major League Baseball, being the biggest sport in North America, allowed racism to control who it allowed on their rosters. Black players did not play in Major League Baseball until Jackie Robinson played first base for the Brooklyn Dodgers on April 15, 1947.

Robinson's path to the league was not always a sure thing, though. As a young man, Robinson briefly struggled. He joined a neighborhood gang for a short time, but thankfully turned away from that life and decided to focus on school and sports.

He did very well in several sports, and he even broke a junior college record in the broad jump. While he was excelling in athletics, he refused to remain quiet on the racism plaguing the country.

Robinson was arrested in 1938 for disputing a detention punishment handed to another Black student, and while he received a two-year suspended sentence, it did hurt his reputation a little bit.

He did not let that stop him though, and he continued breaking records in several sports.

He set the UCLA football record by carrying for 12.2 yards per attempt. He also won the 1940 NCAA Championship in the long jump. He played baseball at the school, too, but his batting average was .097 during the one season he played.

Robinson joined the military but was arrested after refusing what he believed was a racist command. It worked out in his favor, though, as he was acquitted of all charges and honorably discharged without having to see any combat.

Then, while working as an athletic director at Samuel Houston College, he was approached by the Kansas City Monarchs of the Negro Leagues. Robinson accepted, and while he played well, he was upset by the lack of organization from those running the league.

Looking to move up, he pushed for a spot on an MLB team. He got a tryout with the Red Sox, initially, but they did not take him seriously, and it was a humiliating moment for Robinson. However, a few months later, he was approached by the Brooklyn Dodgers, who wanted to interview him. They were concerned about his fiery past, but Robinson began to understand that joining the MLB would require suffering a lot of abuse.

Robinson convinced the Dodgers he could rise above it, and they offered him a contract.

What followed was a very strong career. Robinson would make the All-Star game six times, and he was named National League MVP in 1949. He also won a World Series with the Dodgers in 1955, one year before he stepped away from the game. One World Series may not seem impressive, but in his ten years with the Dodgers, they reached the championship series six times.

Robinson's MLB career was not the longest or most impressive in terms of statistics or trophies, but his presence in Major League Baseball forever changed the sport and the country around him.

# The Cubs' Curse

The Chicago Cubs had not won a World Series since 1908, so when the team reached the 1945 World Series, the people of Chicago were excited for a championship. One fan by the name of William Sianis was quite excited. He tried to attend Game 4 using money he had saved up to purchase box seats, but there was a problem. See, Sianis earned his money working as the owner of the Billy Goat Tavern, and he wanted to bring his pet goat to the game with him.

Well, the stadium staff was not going to allow that, so they sent Sianis and his goat home. As Sianis was leaving the stadium, he allegedly declared the following: "Them Cubs, they ain't gonna win no more."

It did not help things that the Cubs would go on to lose the 1945 World Series in seven games. From there, the rumor of Sianis' curse as he left the stadium that day only grew.

Fans began to take it seriously, and some even tried to break the curse with rituals and prayers, some even involving goats.

Nothing seemed to work, though. The Cubs went another 71 years without a championship, and one particular event in 2003 made it seem as though the team would never win another World Series.

The Cubs were up three games to two in the 2003 National League Championship series, and they were five outs away from reaching the World Series. They were beating the Florida Marlins 3-0 in the game when Marlins batter Luis Castillo hit a ball into the outfield that was going foul. Cubs outfielder Moises Alou chased toward the ball, but when he arrived to make the catch, a fan reached out and caught the ball, preventing the Cubs from getting another out!

The fan, Steve Bartman, became the whipping boy of the cursed Cubs, who went on to lose the NLCS to the Marlins. It was a terrible moment for the team, and it seemed as though the curse would never lift.

It was not until October of 2016, exactly 45 years after the death of William Sianis, that the Cubs won the NLCS against the Dodgers to reach the World Series.

In the 2016 World Series, the Cubs had to defeat the Cleveland Indians if they wanted a chance to end the curse. Game 1 was a bad omen, though, as the Indians won 6-0.

The Cubs responded in Game 2 with a 5-1 win, but they were shut out in a close 1-0 contest, disappointing their home crowd and falling behind in the series. It was even worse when they lost Game 4, falling behind 3-1 in the series.

In Game 5, the Cubs won a close 3-2 game, then they clobbered the Indians 9-3 in Game 6 to force a winner-take-all Game 7.

After a back-and-forth game, the score was tied heading into the ninth inning and remained tied going into the tenth. Ben Zobrist and Miguel Montero both hit RBIs in the tenth for a two-run lead, which the Cubs would preserve and win their first World Series in 108 years.

The curse was finally lifted, so no goats or fans could be blamed anymore.

# The Shot Heard 'Round the World

In 1951, the New York Giants were determined to not allow the regular season to end in a whimper. In the American League, the New York Yankees had opened a sizable lead on their opponents, making their appearance in the World Series a near certainty. In the National League, the Brooklyn Dodgers seemed to be in the process of doing the same.

With 50 games left in the season, the Dodgers were 13.5 games ahead of the Philadelphia Phillies and the Giants. While the Phillies began to fade as the season wound down, the Giants went on a winning streak of 16 games. They were still six games back, but it was progress.

Four weeks later, the Dodgers' lead was down to 4.5 games, but there were only ten games left in the season. It seemed as though the Giants had run out of time. Then, incredibly, they finished their season on a seven-game winning streak while the Dodgers lost six of their last ten. Inexplicably, the two teams had identical records to end the season, meaning a three-game playoff series would determine which of them would represent the National League at the World Series.

Of course, the two teams split the first two games of the series, leaving everything to Game 3. Winner to the World Series, loser goes home.

Well, things did not go well for the Giants throughout the game, and they entered the bottom of the ninth inning trailing the Dodgers by a score of 4-1. However, their offense found a little bit of life, as the first two batters reached base. Then a pop-up put the Giants two outs away from their season's end.

Whitey Lockman doubled to left field, scoring one and advancing another batter to third. With two on, the potential winning run was coming to the plate.

Bobby Thomson walked to the plate, determined to help his team across the line as thousands of people watched around the country.

The first pitch was called a strike, but the second pitch was swung on and hit, a line drive to left field that carried over the wall and ended the game in an instant. Bobby Thomson sent his team to the World Series with a home run called the "Shot Heard 'Round the World."

Dodgers' Jackie Robinson watched as Thomson rounded the bases. Robinson was determined to use the loss as motivation moving forward.

The Giants would go on to lose the World Series in six games, but their arrival to the championship series was a miracle finish by itself, capturing the attention of the country for weeks. Bobby Thomson was a temporary hero, and the game of baseball grew in popularity again.

# Red Sox Down 3-0

It is the 2004 American League Championship Series. The two teams facing each other are the Boston Red Sox and New York Yankees, rivals in every sense of the word. Both squads had been performing well for several years, though the Yankees were often getting the better of their opponents, not to mention the titles that the Yankees had been winning.

And in this series, it looked like the trend would continue. The New York Yankees won the first three games of the series, taking a demanding lead that no other team in baseball history had ever come back from.

It seemed like the Red Sox would add yet another year without a World Series, as the team had not won the title since 1918.

Game 4 appeared as though it would be more of the same, as the Yankees sent their 1999 ALCS MVP pitcher, Orlando Hernandez, to the mount for the start. Even worse, the Yankees jumped out to a 2-0 lead in the third inning.

The Red Sox were determined to fight back, though, scoring three in the fifth inning to take the lead, but it didn't last long. The Yankees responded in the sixth inning with two more runs to retake the lead.

Down to their final three outs, the Red Sox managed to score a run on legendary closer Mariano Rivera, tying the game and sending it to extra innings. Then, in the bottom of the 12th inning, David Ortiz hit a two-run home run to win the game for the Red Sox, extending the series, even if only briefly.

Game 5 required another comeback from the Red Sox, as they were down 4-2 in the bottom of the eighth inning before they scored two runs to tie the game and head to extras once again. This time, the Sox needed 14 innings to win the game, scoring thanks to a single from Ortiz.

Then, in Game 6, Curt Schilling pitched with a bleeding ankle from a torn tendon. The game came to be known as the "Bloody Sock Game," as his injury was quite visible on television. The Sox won that game 4-2, no extra innings needed, setting up an improbable Game 7.

Boston wasted no time in the deciding game, going up 6-0 after two innings and cruising to a 10-3 victory, becoming the first team in MLB history to overcome a 3-0 deficit.

The Red Sox went on to sweep the St. Louis Cardinals in four straight games, winning their first World Series since 1918 and marking the official end of the "Curse of the Bambino."

# The 1998 Home Run Race

During the 1998 Major League Baseball regular season, several players were on pace to break a decades-old record for the number of home runs by one player in a single season. Roger Maris set the record of 61 back in 1961, but it seemed as though the record was ready to fall.

Matt Williams of the Giants, along with Ken Griffey Jr. of the Mariners, were both on pace to break the record in 1994, but the season was shortened. Then, in 1995, Albert Belle reached 50 home runs, and he was only the fourth player to do it in three decades.

Then, Mark McGwire hit 52 home runs despite not playing in 32 of his team's games.

As the 1998 season began, McGwire added to the speculation of the record going down when he hit a home run in each of his first four games. While many thought that Griffey would be in the race to beat the record, it was actually Sammy Sosa of the Cubs who began tracking to be in the race.

McGwire hit 16 home runs in May, leading the league with 27 and setting a pace to hit 80 by the end of the season. Then, in June, Sosa began to catch up to his rival. He had four games in which he hit more than one home run, and he finished the month with 20 added to his total, an MLB record.

Going into July, Sosa and Griffey were tied at 33, both four behind McGwire. At the end of August, both batters were tied at 55, with Griffey trailing behind at 47.

Then, as McGwire got to 60, it just so happened that his next opponent for the next two games would be Sosa and the Cubs.

In the first game, he hit one home run, and then, sure enough, he hit the record-breaking home run in the second game against the Cubs.

Sosa celebrated with McGwire during the moment. Six games later, the two batters were tied at 62. Sosa would finish the season with 66, and McGwire finished with 70. It was a thrilling race that captivated the baseball world, even though the players would eventually admit - or be linked - to the use of steroids.

The same goes for Barry Bonds, who would break the record a few years later. It was a fun time to watch baseball, but would they have gotten there without the cheating?

# A Baseball Quiz

1. Which MLB player has hit more singles than any other player in baseball history?

   A. Pete Rose
   B. Alex Rodriguez
   C. Barry Bonds
   D. Hank Aaron

2. Which slugger holds the MLB record for the most intentional walks, as he was one of the most feared hitters in the league?

   A. Hank Aaron
   B. Barry Bonds
   C. Mark McGwire
   D. Sammy Sosa

3. Which pitcher has more complete games than any other player in history, and it is not particularly close?

   A. Nolan Ryan
   B. Mariano Rivera
   C. Cy Young
   D. Ed Walsh

4. Which clutch batter has hit more grand slams in his career than any other player?

   A. Barry Bonds
   B. Sammy Sosa
   C. Alex Rodriguez
   D. Cecil Fielder

5. Bartolo Colon is the oldest player to hit his first home run. Which team did he play for at the time of his record?

    A. Cleveland Indians
    B. Anaheim Angels
    C. Oakland Athletics
    D. New York Mets

6. The AL and NL career records in RBIs are separated by how many RBIs?

    A. One
    B. 24
    C. 36
    D. 155

7. Which player has stolen more bases than any other player in league history?

    A. Vince Coleman
    B. Ichiro Suzuki
    C. Lou Brock
    D. Rickey Henderson

8. Which pitcher broke the record for most saves in a single season back in 2008?

    A. Eric Gagne
    B. Francisco Rodriguez
    C. Mariano Rivera
    D. John Smoltz

9. Which outfielder holds the MLB record for best fielding percentage with at least 1,000 games played in the outfield?

    A. Shane Victorino
    B. Nick Markakis
    C. Jason Bay

D. Jacoby Ellsbury

10. **Which pitcher has the distinction of having given up the most home runs during his career?**

    A. Frank Tanana
    B. Warren Spahn
    C. Jamie Moyer
    D. Bert Blyleven

# CONCLUSION

There are so many talented athletes in the world, and they all do their best to win for their team, their city, or their country. Sports fans have the pleasure of watching and supporting these athletes and celebrating their successes or mourning their failures.

Sports have become one of the best engines for storytelling in the modern world, emulating the combativeness that war used to occupy so many in ancient times. Now, it can be done much more safely, and competitors can continue to participate for much longer.

Sports give fans the moments they have always dreamed of seeing, or they break hearts and ask the fans to wait one more season. Either way, folks are happy and entertained.

This book covered several of the major sports that occupy the hearts and minds of people around the world. Each chapter examined some of the biggest names and most incredible stories, all while delivering information in the form of quick facts or entertaining tales. The quiz questions made sure you are aware of how much you know - or do not!

The great part is that you likely learned something you didn't know. Even better is that many of these stories have much more detail and depth, just begging to be explored. The world of sports is always ready to tell another great story, but you have to go and find it!

After all, you can't experience every big moment in every sport as they happen. You have to look back and relive those moments so you can pass them on to friends and family. If there is a story you thought was interesting in this book, then research it more so you can experience every little detail of these epic moments!

Keep sporting and supporting your favorite athletes!

# SOLUTIONS

## World Championships

1. C. 400 meters and 800 meters. Her records are some of the oldest records in the history books.
2. A. Oscar Schmidt. He averaged 34.6 points for Brazil during the 1990 iteration of the event.
3. B. Mexico. They have collected 28 losses in 17 appearances at World Cup tournaments.
4. D. Germany. They also have four titles, which is more than the Netherlands, who have three finals losses and zero titles.
5. A. Vladislav Tretiak. He collected ten golds, two silvers, and one bronze from 1970 to 1983.
6. B. Daisuke Matsuzaka. He was named the MVP in both the 2006 and 2009 iterations of the tournament.
7. D. Michael Phelps. He also leads the world with 26 gold medals, which he collected from 2001 to 2011.
8. B. 1995. His jump of 18.29 meters added 0.13 meters to his previous record.
9. C. Badminton. The Thomas Cup, or World Men's Team Championships, have been held every two years since 1982, and every three years from 1948–49 to 1982.
10. A. Australia. They have won 75.48% of their matches. India is in second with 67.55%.

# Tennis

1. B. Pineapple. Accounts differ on the reason why a pineapple rests on top of the trophy, though. Some think it was a symbol of luxury, and others think it was a great compliment to receive one because they could not be imported to grow in the United Kingdom.
2. A. Black or white. The two colors were interchangeable depending on the color of the playing surface at the time. Yellow was not introduced as a color for tennis balls until 1972, to help television viewers see the ball.
3. C. Three. The 11-hour, five-minute match had to be split up between three days of competition.
4. C. 263 km/h. Sam Groth achieved the feat in May 2012. However, he lost the match in which he accomplished the feat.
5. D. 64. It was only reinstated in 1988. Today, the Olympics also include men's and women's doubles, along with mixed doubles.
6. B. Clay. Many consider Rafael Nadal the King of Clay, but Chris Evert's record is untouched by any other man or woman in the history of the sport.
7. A. James I of Scotland. He tried to escape through a privy, but he had ordered the privy drain hole closed to stop his tennis balls from rolling into it.
8. B. Rafael Nadal. He has 14 French Open titles. Bjorn Borg is next closest in the Open Era with six.
9. A. Martina Navratilova. She won the tournament nine times, two more than Steffi Graf and Serena Williams.
10. D. Bjorn Borg. Agassi noticed that Borg's tongue would unintentionally indicate where he was about to place his serve. Agassi used this to his advantage to beat Borg, only telling him about it years later.

# Boxing and MMA

1. A. Rocky Marciano. He finished his career with a 49-0 record, which included an impressive 43 knockouts. He was the lineal champion from 1952 to 1955.
2. B. Joe Louis. The arena was used to host professional hockey games until April 2017.
3. D. Bernard Hopkins. He won the WBC and lineal heavyweight titles at age 46, breaking a record previously held by George Foreman.
4. A. Oscar De La Hoya. He earned the nickname after winning gold at the 1992 Summer Olympics. It also helped that he's one of the highest-grossing boxers of all time.
5. D. 24. She won every professional match in her career, collecting 21 knockouts, while she won four belts at super middleweight and one at light heavyweight.
6. A. Jon Jones. He has competed in 16 total title fights. Couture and St-Pierre each have 15, and Johnson has 14. He's also the only one of the four to be undefeated in those fights.
7. D. Jim Miller. He has 26 wins across three weight classes. Arlovski and Cerrone are next on the list with 23, and Poirier has 22.
8. C. Anderson Silva. His nine finishes in title bouts are one more than Hughes, two more than Johnson, and three more than Rousey.
9. D. Conor McGregor. He knocked out Jose Aldo in 13 seconds at UFC 194.
10. D. Demetrious Johnson. He defeated Kyoji Horiguchi by armbar in UFC 186.

## Ice Hockey

1. A. Montreal Canadiens. The Canadiens have 35 appearances in the Finals. Edmonton and Philadelphia are tied at eight for most among non-Original six teams.
2. B. Mike Bossy. He had nine 50-goal seasons in ten years with the Islanders.
3. C. Patrick Marleau. He played all those games for San Jose, Toronto, and Pittsburgh.
4. D. Aleksandr Ryazantsev. He hit a shot at 114.127 miles per hour in 2012.
5. D. Nine. There are five spots in the neutral zone and two in each offensive end.
6. B. Three. It is only one inch thick, though.
7. B. Jacques Plante. He started wearing it in 1959 after taking a shot to the face from Andy Bathgate of the New York Rangers. His coach, Toe Blake, initially did not want him to wear the mask, fearing it would obstruct his vision.
8. A. Score a goal. The puck is often referred to as the biscuit because they are similar shapes.
9. C. Florida Panthers. It was all because of a 1995 story that came out in the press detailing how the Panthers' captain, Scott Mellanby, killed a rat that appeared in the team's locker room.
10. D. Boston Bruins. They've lost the Finals series 14 times, a tragic record on the biggest stage in the sport.

## Basketball

1. D. Dwight Howard. He is the only player to win three DPOY awards, while several players have collected two.
2. B. 33. They accomplished the feat during the 1971–72 season, losing to the Bucks to end the streak.
3. B. Michael Jordan. He accomplished the feat during the 1987–88 season, which was only his fourth year in the NBA.
4. A. 35. He was 35 and 284 days old at the exact moment of receiving the award.
5. C. Vince Carter. His 22 seasons in the NBA is also a record, and he had a great career during those years.
6. C. Seven. Jordan's streak started in 1986, and Wilt's began in 1959.
7. D. Kobe Bryant. Though, he is more remembered for the many shots he made.
8. D. Ten. He was often very close to the basket, which can make shooting, or dunking, a bit easier than jump shots.
9. A. John Stockton. He had 15,806 assists, and Jason Kidd is in second place with 12,091. Chris Paul is nearing 12,000 as of 2023, and LeBron James is just over 11,000.
10. B. Hakeem Olajuwon. He had 3,830 blocks, and he averaged 3.09 blocks per game. Only Mark Eaton and Manute Bol averaged more per game.

# European Football

1. B. Lionel Messi. He scored 91 goals in 69 matches during the 2012 calendar year.
2. C. 1,390. He played for 31 seasons as a goalkeeper.
3. A. Toni Kroos. He won the Champions League six times, the UEFA Super Cup four times, and the FIFA Club World Cup six times.
4. D. Sergio Ramos. He won 131 international matches as a member of the Spanish national team.
5. C. Sheffield. The club was created before the rules of the sport were even finalized.
6. D. 56. The previous record was set in 2005 at 48.
7. A. 31. The New Saints of the Cymru Premier won 26 straight matches in 2023–24.
8. D. 85. The run started in February of 2020, ending in October of 2021.
9. A. Neymar. His transfer fee was 222 million Euros, while Mbappe was transferred for 180 million Euros.
10. B. Turkey. He scored the goal against South Korea, breaking a record from 1962, when a goal was scored in 16 seconds.

## American Football

1.  C. Detroit Lions. He played 21 seasons from 1992 to 2012.
2.  D. Mike Hart. He had 1,005 rushing attempts from 2004 to 2008, and he never lost a fumble.
3.  B. Navy. He had 88 rushing touchdowns from 2012 to 2015, more than any other player of any position in the FBS.
4.  A. Jerry Rice. Though he played for three different teams in the NFL, he spent the majority of his career in San Francisco.
5.  D. Baltimore Ravens. He made a 66-yard field goal against the Detroit Lions.
6.  C. 16. His record spanned from 2005 to 2020, where he played for five different teams.
7.  D. Barry Sanders. He rushed for 1,883 yards without a fumble during the 1994 season.
8.  C. Patrick Mahomes. Both players threw for 734 yards, Halliday in 2014 and Mahomes in 2016.
9.  A. Case Keenum. He threw 155 touchdown passes from 2007 to 2011.
10. B. 54. His record ran from 2009 to 2012.

# Baseball

1. A. Pete Rose. He collected 3,215 singles and 4,256 hits while playing for four teams from 1963 to 1986.
2. B. Barry Bonds. He was intentionally walked 688 times in his career, as many pitchers did not want to risk giving up a home run.
3. C. Cy Young. He had 749 complete games throughout his career, and Pud Galvin is more than 100 behind him for second place on the list.
4. C. Alex Rodriguez. He hit 25 grand slams during his career in Major League Baseball.
5. D. New York Mets. He was 42 years and 349 days old at the time of his first home run.
6. A. 1. Hank Aaron had a total of 2,297 RBIs, but only 2,202 of those came in the National League. Babe Ruth holds the AL record with 2,201 RBIs.
7. D. Rickey Henderson. He had 1,406 steals with nine different teams during his career.
8. B. Francisco Rodriguez. He had 62 saves while pitching for Los Angeles that season.
9. A. Shane Victorino. His percentage was .996 while playing with San Diego, Philadelphia, and Los Angeles.
10. C. Jamie Moyer. He gave up 522 home runs during his time with eight different teams. He gave up the most while playing with Seattle.

Made in the USA
Columbia, SC
17 December 2024

49486878R00098